My Body Is The Temple

Encounters and Revelations of Sacred Dance and Artistry

By Rev. Stephanie Butler

xulon PRESS

Xulon Press
11350 Random Hills Road
Suite 800
Fairfax, VA 22030
(703) 279-6511
XulonPress.com

To order additional copies, call 1-866-909-BOOK (2665).

Dedication

This book is my love offering to the One who is my Everything. It is what I call my 'reasonable service', that is, my 'spiritual act of worship'. It is You, Father, who formed me in my mother's womb; it is You who watched over me as a child and it is You who removed the scales from my eyes and called me to a life of holiness, purity, freedom, and joy! How proud I am to be Your daughter! Lord, may my life be a continual praise unto You.

To my fellow ministers, students, awesomely anointed colleagues in sacred artistry, my circle of intercessors, the 'trinity connection' in Jamaica—much, much love and appreciation to all of you. Thank you Josie for your ministry to MY FEET. Deb, thank you for pointing me to The Way. May each of us continue to honor the Father with our bodies, uncompromisingly bringing Him glory in all our hands find to do.

Acknowledgements

To my beloved mother and friend, Mary Ernell Butler: you are a phenomenal woman. Your courage and strength in the face of adversity has been imparted into my spirit eternally. Thank you for your sacrificial and unconditional love poured out over my life. You are the wind beneath my wings.

To my sisters and brothers: what a family! Full of variety, excitement, joy and triumph. Thank you for teaching, defending, protecting, and loving me. Each of you has a special place in my heart. I pray that you will discover the true power and potential that God has placed inside of you to live a victorious, prosperous life in Jesus Christ.

To my spiritual mothers, Rev. Dr. Cecelia Williams Bryant and Dr. Patricia Morgan: words cannot express the love, respect, and appreciation God has placed in my heart towards the two of you. You have assisted the Holy Spirit in shaping and forming me into a daughter of destiny and a princess of the nations. Thank you for demonstrating excellence before me, both publicly and privately. Wherever I am in the world, I will always connect with you in the Spirit. I love you dearly.

To Bishop John Richard Bryant and Dr. Peter Morgan:

true men of wisdom, class, charisma, and integrity. Thank you so very much for all that you have imparted to me through solid, Spirit-filled teaching and for your commitment to justice, love for family, ministry to the disadvantaged, and empowerment of nations to bring about change in the world.

Contents

Contents

Foreword

Hear the heart of GOD you Servants of the LORD!

Allow fresh streams of REVELATION to outflow your worship.

Ascend to the depths of His Glorious Majesty.

Partake of morsels of Divinity soaked in prayer and suffering LOVE.

Cross the "BRIDGE" to a new self and a new self-understanding.

Cross the BRIDGE and enter the place of TRINITARIAN experience.

Cross the BRIDGE while shedding the mind shackles, the body shame and the spirit darkness of past life oppressions, sin, and fear.

Cross the BRIDGE and consent to your Dream manna, your winged gifts of prophecy, healing, intercession, and JOY *unsearchable*.

THIS is the missing dimension.

THIS is the long-awaited *unfoldment*.

THIS is the next step! Lift UP your feet.

Let all Believers in the Divine Sonship and Sacred Lordship, and Holy Messiahship of JESUS CHRIST Now Come!

Let the Papacy come. The Apostles Come!

Let the Cardinals and Bishops Come!

Let all Elders and Pastors and Teachers Come!

Let the Missionaries Come!

The Exhorters and New Believers Come! Come Boldly. Come Broken. Come Betrothed to the Lamb of the Dance!

This Stephanie, this Oracle of the Dance, Her "Body is the Temple". Her mind is the "Temple". Her Soul is the "Temple". And such can be true of each of us. Only position yourself to be taught.

Position yourself to wait in the PRESENCE OF THE LORD. Be open to a radicalized Global view of your "Call". Prepare to experience the dissolution of the Spirit-Body dichotomy familiar to us as we minister, pray, witness, and study. There will come unanticipated BREAKTHROUGHS as you seek to know the heart of GOD. As you consent to realized impartation! As you set aside the "former things"—success, failure, fame, approval, rejection—God's "new thing" begins in you.

This is WISDOM. The WISDOM that was in the Beginning. The WISDOM of the High GOD, Most Holy and Eternal. In WISDOM, the NOW explodes and exults and ignites until the Soul can but DANCE. It is a Dance that rebukes the nations. It is a Dance of Healing and Hope. Visions and Prophesies. It is the dynamic tension of a New World being born. It is a Dance of Holy feet ablaze with prophecy. It is a Dance of the unknowable, intangible, irrevocable song of GOD! And we are amazed, slain, compelled, drawn, taken, humbled, convicted, repentant, excited, forgiven, endued, and inebriated until Glory Halleluia! "Swoosh"!

Rev. Dr. Cecelia Williams Bryant
Author and Founder, AKOSUA Visions Global
Ministries
Episcopal Supervisor, 5th District African Methodist
Episcopal Church

Introduction

***M**y Body Is The Temple: Encounters and Revelations of Sacred Dance and Artistry* is at once the author's sacrifice of her body to her God, as it is an artistic expression of her willingness to share the mysteries of total obedience that she has gained. That commitment, to the ministry of dance and of shaping the church and the Nations through the sacred and performing arts, is lavishly passed on to her readers.

The following volume is as much an 'Ave Maria' of striking devotion to God, as it is closely reminiscent of Mary's own "Be it (done) unto me according to thy Word." The response of the Mother of Jesus to the proposition of God offered through the angel- messenger—to bear in her body the Son of God, and to make her own body the very Temple of God, is captured repeatedly in the pages of this volume. The demand on the reader seems to necessarily be that of a response to the eternal proposition, "Will you let your body become a temple which I can indwell?" And through which I myself can express My own Divinity and expose My pent-up Glory?

My Body Is The Temple is incarnate in its nature and offers to every reader the opportunity to comprehend how the WORD can become flesh and dwell within the body of man. It further explains how through the body, that Word, which shatters darkness and delivers nations, is to be given release aggressively, forcefully, and strategically to accomplish the purpose for which it was sent. The totality of the response is where the appeal is. It is demanding, as it is appealing. The privilege extended to the reader is that of 'inscaping' the heart and soul of the author and of learning from her most private experiences with her God and from her public ministry to the Nations.

I am honored to witness in the life of this artist, her ministry gift to the world. And through it the mystery of creation, the reciprocal mutuality of the created with the Creator, and the revelation of the truth of Divine Condescension—to dwell within the created body, this temple, her life is one of the finest revelatory works on the subject of which she writes. I am proud to partake of that revealed glory!

Dr. Patricia Morgan
Author, Educational Psychologist
Morgan Ministries International
Jamaica, West Indies

Terminology Background

What compels us to dance? For some, it is a natural, outward manifestation of an internal rhythmic unction—that which has been present in the souls of men and women since before they were formed in their mother's womb. For others, dance is the free, liberating expression of movement through the embracing of diasporic roots and culture. For yet others, dance is a legal opportunity to showcase the body in order to enhance, promote, or sell an agenda with a message of sexuality, sensuality, and eroticism.

However, what compels us, as Liturgical Dance Ministers, to movement is the knowledge that our very lives must be worship unto the Lord Jesus Christ to the glory of God the Father. We purpose in our hearts to use our gifts, skills, and abilities in sacred artistry according to the Truth of His Word. Romans Chapter 12:1 commands us to present our bodies as a living sacrifice, holy and acceptable unto Him which is our "spiritual act of worship". This worship includes the sacrifice of praise manifested in the dance.

Regardless of one's title, position, office, degree, or level of gifting, every action of the body, when done as unto the Lord, IS an act of worship! Therefore, it is through the use of teachings, affirmations, prayer declarations, prophecies, and revelations that this book declares that all of us are called to dance. Yet, only a unique and chosen lot is called to the Sacred and Liturgical Dance Ministry.

The invitation to journey through the pages that follow is extended to whosoever will—no one is excluded.

Sacred and Liturgical Dance

In the section entitled 'Liturgical Dance', we will explore the philosophy of the call to dance. We will discover the significance and criticality of keeping one's entire body whole, healthy, and holy before God in order to fulfill our destiny and to execute His plan for us. We will address strongholds, perceptions, stereotypes, and motives surrounding the sacred and liturgical dance ministry as viewed by the Church and the secular community.

By building a strategic foundation of knowledge, wisdom, and cutting edge creative concepts, the Holy Spirit will provide divine insight into the gift of dance, which God has given His people as effective weapons of praise, warfare, deliverance, healing, and joy. This foundation then becomes the platform by which men, women, and children will arise as global leaders and revolutionaries in the restoration and sanctification of Sacred Arts to the Church Universal.

Prophetic Dance

In the section on Prophetic Dance in Worship, you will obtain revelatory understanding of the three key purposes for the gift of prophecy and how the Holy Spirit through the prophetic dance experience activates these purposes. You will also discover how to identify and interpret the prophetic content of your dreams and visions through the application of biblical revelatory principles designed to extract and prophesy "movement messages" to the Nations and the Church. The results of these messages are 'Prophetic Declarations' which the dancer brings forth via the spoken Word and in the body before the congregation.

Affirmations, Prayer Declarations, and Revelations

Throughout this text, there are collections of sacred affirmations, prayer declarations, and revelations. The significance and strength of these statements will provide understanding and insight into the various stages of the author's conversion experience and life as one who has been radically transformed by the supernatural healing power of Dance.

Sacred Affirmations

The word 'affirm' means to build up, encourage, proclaim and declare through words that strengthen one's soul. It means to speak life into one's spirit and to bring focus to the inner-gifting of a person through verbal confession. By speaking words of affirmation, we are empowered to aggressively attack and lay hold of that for which God already has positioned us. We speak and believe that we are who God says we are.

Sacred Affirmations became a source of life to me several years ago. Curled up on the living room floor of my home with shades drawn, I traveled daily with the enemy deeper and deeper into a darkness of depression, isolation, and condemnation. This season came after a series of devastating blows to my personal life and my health. The assignment of the spirit of depression is to force its victims into a state of deadly silence and numbness. It was in that place of silence, that I heard the faint 'swoosh' of the river inside of me—There was still life to draw upon. It was here that the Holy Spirit birthed the dance IN my belly. I was silenced and numb, but in between the enemy's footsteps, I HEARD the Word of God in the *movement* of the water! Gradually, I was able to write the 'Word-Dance' that was manifested in my spirit. These words became **Dances of Affirmation**.

It is these same affirmations that the Holy Spirit used to REVIVE and HEAL me. They taught me how to dance IN the fire, to dance DURING my wilderness, and to restore the JOY of my Salvation. Each chapter will begin with Sacred Affirmations. Meditate on them. Speak and BELIEVE them. Write your own affirmations and allow them to illuminate your soul!

The *INVOCATION*

"Enter the Rhythm"

Enter the rhythm of God's timing;
The rhythm that propels your dead, lifeless groans
into uncontrollable cries and shouts of praise.

Enter the rhythm of God's timing-
The rhythm that takes your soul from here to there;
from there to there—in an instant, seizing every God-given
    moment;
No time to waste.

Enter the rhythm that only hears the snapping fingers of the
    Holy Spirit
in tune with an angelic orchestra, while God unrelentlessly
    beats
upon African drums with Caribbean zeal;
Move... Run... Dance! FLY!

Enter the rhythm of God's timing and be made Whole;
When His timing FREES you from the expectations of
    others;

When His timing whispers to your soul, "Liberation Time is
    Here!"
and before you know it, you're caught up in the rapture of
    His love.

Enter the rhythm of God's timing and experience an authen-
    tic anointing;
No need to make one up;
To fake one up;
It's yours! Yours for the asking!
Ask and it will be given to you;
Seek and you will find;
Knock and the doors will be OPENED unto you! Wow! I
    See a River of Open DOORS...
You could see them too if you are WILLING to
OPEN yourself to the rhythm of NOW.

Yesterday is gone,
But GOD is swaying...NOW;
GOD is singing...NOW!
GOD is marching...NOW!
GOD is dancing...NOW!

And then the LORD inquires:
"But who will consecrate themselves today before Me?
Who will hold tightly to My hands as we whirl across the
    Nations?
Who will receive the gentle touch of My right hand on their
    shoulder,
and My left arm around their waist? I long for you to put
    your tiny feet upon Mine,
and let ME lead the dance as only a True Father can!

If you will enter the rhythm of My timing, I will sing to you
    a New Song so sweet:

"You are the Sunshine of My life, that's why I'll ALWAYS
    be around..."
Shine for Me and I will transform you;
Shine for Me and You will be My Seed to the Nations...

But whom shall I send? Who will go for Us?
Whose feet can be trusted to deliver the Truth?
Whose feet are fit to RUN with the flask of oil
that fills the jars of the oppressed?
Whose feet will POUNCE joyfully with warrior-like preci-
    sion
into the kingdom of darkness and
PROPHESY until deliverance is Manifested?
Whose feet will teach the children of the World to dance
a Dance of Purity unto Me"?

And I Replied:
MY FEET, Father!
The Nations await MY FEET;
MY FEET will *travel* all the Earth;
MY FEET will *see* many lives transformed into the
Glorious liberty of our LORD JESUS Christ;
MY FEET will *bring* restoration to many;
MY FEET will *reach* the Unreached;
MY FEET are Anointed to *carry* the Good News of the
    Gospel of Peace;
MY FEET are as Alabaster Boxes *waiting* to be broken;
Here Am I, Lord— Send Me!
MY FEET WILL GO!

Sacred AFFIRMATION #1

I AM NOT insane!
I AM who GOD says I am!
I AM BORN for <u>This</u> Time!
I WILL Preserve My Wholeness of Self!

CHAPTER ONE

My Body Is The Temple: Preparing for the Indwelling

1Cor. 6:19: "Or do you not know that your body is the temple of the Holy Spirit who is IN you and you are not your own. You were bought with a price, therefore, glorify God with your WHOLE body, and your spirit which are God's. (NIV)

The Body is the physical part of a human, distinct from the spiritual. The Body is also referred to as the Church of Jesus Christ. All Believers are Members of the Body—together we are one Body with many different parts. A Temple is a house or a dwelling place of God. It is that which has been erected and set apart for worship of the true and living God. The Temple that King Solomon built for the Lord to dwell in was created to be a "wonder to the whole world"!

In preparing our body-temples for the indwelling of the Holy Spirit, there is a revelation that the sacred dancer must grasp: Our bodies, and what we DO with them are designed to be a WONDER to the World. As in the temple that

Solomon built, God has erected and set our bodies apart for worship of the true and living God. If our bodies are designed to be a wonder that means that our bodies are LIVING MIRACLES. The human body is a miraculous, resilient work of art. It was designed by God to be an 'extraordinary happening' in the Heavenlies! Of all that God created, our bodies are His prized-possession. It is the most intricately made and finely tuned instrument ever known to man. If we are to assume our positioning in the Kingdom as sacred dancers, we must embrace the reality that we are called to bring healing, salvation, prophetic revelation and JOY to the World through the sacred use of our BODIES.

However, none of this can be realized until the dancer receives full revelation of the necessity and preparation required for this indwelling.

The Holy Spirit's ability to dwell within the body is highly dependent upon two factors: reign and occupancy. 1Corinthians 6:19 reminds Believers that the Holy Spirit is 'in you'. He is not just in one's physical tabernacle being held captive as a caged bird, rather He is in the very fiber of one's being. The Holy Spirit actually occupies our personalities! When He enters in, He seeks a place where He alone can rule and reign in authority. One does not co-habitat, co-counsel, or 'shack up' with the Holy Spirit. He is all encompassing and must occupy that which God has obtained by purchase through the shed blood of His Son Jesus Christ. The understanding of the Holy Spirit's occupancy in our bodies can either be determined by ownership or covenant agreement—both of which God has already accomplished. Therefore, we are not our own—we are ***His own***.

God's chosen Sacred Dancers are commanded to eliminate from their lives anything and everything that defiles the body. This can become very complex in that even those sins committed 'outside' of the body are spiritual manifestations of a deeply rooted inward lack and brokeness.

As a result, the dancer—whether sacred or secular, attracts a variety of spirits which also seek a place to dwell and if one is not careful, that place may be within them! Dance ministers must be able to speak out candidly about their past and present issues of deliverance in order to release themselves from condemnation and to serve as a testimony to others.

During my early years as a new Believer, I struggled to find balance in this area. I realized that there were many habits that I would eventually need to cease, however, I had no strong convictions concerning drinking alcohol, going to nightclubs, watching adult movies, and even fornication—especially if the relationship was monogamous. I also continued to dance professionally in the secular world, where I was regularly exposed to a variety of ungodly practices. I did not believe that my newfound relationship with Jesus Christ disqualified me from continuing in my indulgent lifestyle. Then one evening as I sat relaxing in the tub—Bible in one hand, tall glass of wine in the other, the Holy Spirit caused my eyes to find this scripture in 1Corinthians 6:9:

> **"Neither the sexually immoral, nor idolaters, nor adulterers, nor prostitutes, nor homosexual offenders, nor thieves, nor the greedy, nor drunkards, nor slanderers and swindlers will inherit the Kingdom of God. And that is what some of you were. But you were washed, you were sanctified and you were justified in the name of the Lord Jesus Christ and by the Holy Spirit of God." (NIV)**

When I read further down, I saw in verse 13, **"The body is not meant for sexual immorality, but for the Lord, and the Lord is meant for the body."** I could not take my eyes off this scripture. As I kept reading it repeatedly, I felt a stirring in my heart. The scales were being removed from my eyes. I had the very uncomfortable feeling that at that very moment, God was in the room with me—watching, teaching, and literally cleansing me! "The body is for the Lord, and the Lord for the body" became a seed planted deep within my spirit. Without truly understanding, I knew that I had received a supernatural visitation similar to that of the Virgin Mary when the Holy Spirit 'moved upon' her to conceive our Savior. While my visitation did not produce a human being, it did bring forth and birth a 'holy thing' inside of me! My Call to consecration had arrived. **This** was the beginning of MY **indwelling.**

Revelation:
Your Visitation will arrive when you least expect it, but when God most needs it.
Its purpose: to press you forth towards the next dimension in Him.

God is vitally concerned about what we do, where we go, and how we steward **His Body.** This concern affects us both individually and collectively as The Church. You and I are indeed the Body of Christ. As dance ministers, pastors, and church leaders, we have a right to know the 'whereabouts' of our Body parts and call them to accountability. Therefore, it is unacceptable for **my** saved, unmarried **hips** to be having an affair in Spain, while at the same time, **your** saved, sanctified **hands** are feeding the homeless in Detroit! Nor can **my** born-again, consecrated **lips** get high on marijuana, while you, as a Believer, use **your mouth** to over-indulge in eating or starvation.

Sacred Artists and leaders must be able to stand naked and unashamed before a Holy God if He is to launch you into the fullness of your purpose. The Indwelling of the

Holy Spirit is what truly makes our lives as Believers a wonder to the World. In the preparation and purification process of the indwelling, the dance minister must grow accustomed to viewing the Body-Temple in 3 parts: mind, body, spirit. Our minds, bodies, and spirits must be morally and spiritually excellent, in complete reverence to the Lord.

This is a true, holistic approach to holiness.

In this holistic approach, the individual must invite the Spirit of God to treat the *whole* person, rather than the mere *symptoms* of their disease, dysfunction, or emotional brokenness. For example, to the dance minister, the **symptoms** of his or her emotional brokenness may be an inability to ever **fully** give themselves over to the dance in worship, expression, and adoration of God. This symptom may manifest through an individual who ministers in dance with a blank facial expression, exceptional technique, but lacks impact, energy, and anointing. This kind of display frequently leaves the observer unmoved and unchanged. However, in considering the **whole** person in this scenario, one finds that in general, this dancer's demonstration is actually an out growth of their general personality and demeanor. This demeanor could stem from a childhood of strict discipline and general quietness. As a result of always being told that they should be 'seen and not heard', creative expression of any kind may have never been nurtured nor encouraged in their life.

Revelation:

I must welcome the Holy Spirit of God to have a holistic encounter in every diseased and dysfunctional area of my life no matter how much it hurts. I will be made whole and through my wholeness, others will be healed.

This person, who now finds him or herself, saved and involved in Sacred Arts Ministry has suffered from a form of emotional and psychological abuse, which has succeeded in stunting their ability to express themselves artistically. Why has God now called them to Dance Ministry? Because He knows that as they dance, they will be healed and made whole!

The mind, body, and spirit must all be on one accord. If any one of these is out of order, the enemy will gain access in that area of your life. Not only will you be delayed in fulfilling the plan that God has in store for you, but also you will find yourself weak and defenseless in crucial times of spiritual battle. As you meditate on the following scriptures, ask the Holy Spirit to ACTIVATE your Body-Temple to receive understanding, impartation, anointing, and strategies for warfare against the enemy:

MIND Scriptures:

Isaiah 26:3-4:

You will keep in perfect peace him whose mind is steadfast, because he trusts in you. Trust in the Lord forever, for the Lord is the Rock Eternal.

Romans 7:22-23:

For in my inner being, I delight in God's law, but I see another law at work in the members of my body, waging war against the law of my mind and making me a prisoner of the law of sin which is at work within my members.

Romans 8:6-7:

The mind of a sinful man is death, but the mind controlled by the Spirit is life and peace; the sinful mind is hostile to God, it does not submit to God's law nor can it do so.

Romans 12:2:

Do not be conformed any longer to the patterns of this world, but be transformed by the renewing of your mind.

Acts 20:19:

I served the Lord with great humility and with tears, although my mind was severely tested by the plots of the Jews.

Matthew 22:37-38:

Jesus replied: Love the Lord your God with all your heart and with all your soul and with all your mind. This is the first and greatest commandment.

1John 4:18:

There is no fear in love. But perfect love drives out all fear.

BODY Scriptures:

Genesis 2:7:

And the Lord God formed the man from the dust of the ground and breathed into his nostrils the breath of life, and the man became a living being.

Matthew 26:26:

While they were eating, Jesus took bread, gave thanks, and broke it; he gave it to His disciples, saying, "Take and eat. This is my body."

Romans 6:12-13:

Therefore, do not let sin reign in your mortal body so that you obey its evil desires. Do not offer the parts of your body to sin as instruments of wickedness, but rather offer yourselves to God as those who have been brought from death to life; and offer the parts of your body to Him as instruments of righteousness.

Romans 12:1:

Therefore I urge you, in view of God's mercy, to offer your bodies as living sacrifices; holy and acceptable to God—this is your spiritual act of worship.

I Corinthians 6:18-19:

Flee from sexual immorality. All other sins a man commits are outside his body, but he who sins sexually sins against his own body. Or do you not know that your body is the temple of the Holy Spirit, who is in you, whom you have received from God? You are not your own. You were bought with a price. Therefore, honor God with your body.

IIIJohn v.2:

Beloved, I pray among all things that you may enjoy good health [in your body] and prosper even as your soul does prosper.

SPIRIT Scriptures:

Deut. 30:9-10:

The Lord will again delight in you and make you prosperous, just as he delighted in your fathers; if you obey the Lord your God and keep his commands and decrees that are written in this Book of the Law and turn to the

Lord your God with all your heart and with all your soul.

Joshua 22:5:

But be very careful to keep the commandment and the law that Moses the servant of the Lord your God, to walk in all His ways, to obey his commands, to hold fast to him and to serve him with all your heart and all your soul.

IKings 2:3-4:

Walk in His ways and keep his decrees and commands, his laws and requirements, as written in the Law of Moses so that you may prosper in all you do and wherever you go; that the Lord may keep His promise to me: "If your descendants watch how they live, and if they walk faithfully before me with all their heart and soul, you will never fail to have a man on the throne of Israel…"

John 4:23-24:

Yet a time is coming and has now come when the true worshippers will worship the Father in spirit and in truth, for they are the kind of worshippers that the Lord seeks. God is Spirit and His worshippers must worship in spirit and in truth.

IJohn 4:1-3:

Dear Friends, do not believe every spirit, but test the spirits to see whether they are from God; because many false prophets have gone out into the world. This is how you can recognize the Spirit of God: every spirit that does not acknowledge Jesus is not from God.

The indwelling of the Holy Spirit in each one of us is vital to the maintenance of our Kingdom authority given to us by our Lord Jesus Christ. As we make our body-temples ready for worship and warfare through the revelation of the Word, God will equip and strengthen us as ministers and sacred artists who are on the pathway to spiritual balance, Godly health, happiness, and wholeness— both inwardly and outwardly.

Prayer Declaration:

Holy Father,
As I lift my hands to You, I declare that this is my body.
My body is the temple of the Holy Spirit;
Lord, I glorify you for giving me such a gift to be used in worship, warfare, and healing to Your people.
I speak to my mind, my body, and my spirit in the Name of the Lord Jesus Christ and say,
"Line up! Come into obedience and harmony with God's perfect order, NOW!"
I believe it and thank You for speedy manifestation in Jesus' Name,
Amen.

Reader's Reflections:

(Fill in your own personal statements of affirmation.)

My Affirmations:

I Am _____

_____

_____

Right Now, I Must _____

_____

_____

I Declare _____

_____

_____

Sacred AFFIRMATION #2

My JOY Has the Power to Heal!

My LAUGHTER Shakes the kingdom of Darkness!

My DANCE Is the Embodiment of New Wine and the Oil of Gladness!

My CELEBRATION Will Bring Transformation!

My CHANGE WILL Come!

CHAPTER TWO

The JOY of the LORD Is Strength to the Body

...And Ezra the priest and teacher said to them, "This day is holy to the LORD. Do not be grieved nor depressed, for the joy of the Lord is your strength and stronghold." Nehemiah 8:10, (Amplified)

Experiencing true joy in the Lord is a mighty weapon of warfare and an instrument of peace given to us by God for two key purposes:

1) To assist in bringing a sense of LIFE, PURITY, Holiness and balance to our mind, body, and spirit.

2) To target, attack, pull-down, and DESTROY the plans of satan in our personal lives and in the world

How can something so seemingly simple accomplish such an awesome task? 1Corinthians 10:2 says, "The weapons of our warfare are not of this World but are mighty through God to the pulling down of strongholds". While the scripture saying "the joy of the Lord is our strength" is aimed at us as Believers, it is we who are the ones yet to experience true victory in the area of Joy in our lives. The enemy has many simple and subtle ways of defeating us in the area of joy. Consider this as a 'starter' list:

- I hardly ever smile unless someone smiles at me first
- I don't usually go 24 hours without criticizing something or someone
- I bypass any opportunity to exercise, no matter how slight
- I have a testimony, but less than five people know it
- During Worship, I will clap, but that's basically it
- It is rare that I will give or receive a sincere hug from anyone
- Children do not usually like being in my presence, nor I in theirs

If you answered in the affirmative to any one or more of these statements, you are not taking full advantage of some of the wonderful ways in which God has provided a release and outlet for you to receive joy.

Rejoice in the LORD Always, and Again I say REJOICE!

What does it mean to rejoice? It does not mean what we have typically been taught. In the original Hebrew, the word for rejoice is 'gil'. This literally means to leap, jump, spring about, and whirl. To 'rejoice' does not simply mean to be happy or joyful. It is actually to CELEBRATE IN the act of JOY. When we celebrate there is a natural movement that is manifested. Rejoicing then for the sacred dancer is two things: 1) it is a form of praise unto the Lord and 2) it is a celebratory manifestation of what the inner spirit is doing. The realization is that the Holy Spirit is "making merry" on the inside of us! This is truly what will sustain the sacred dancer and allow us to laugh in the face of adversity and at the tactics of the enemy! Nehemiah 8:10 tells us that we ought not to not grieve, rather to enjoy all that God blesses us with because "the joy of the Lord is our strength"!

Your Body Must Rejoice!

Our Bodies were meant for REJOICING in dance and movement to the Lord. Physical exercise, good health, and happiness are absolutely vital to the human anatomy. Proverbs 17:22 says, "A cheerful heart is good medicine, but a crushed spirit dries up the bones". The implication here is that joy maintains LIFE in the body. As we visualize the human anatomy, we must allow ourselves to supernaturally extend 'laser vision' into the bones. Everything that wraps around the bones is for their own protection. As the blood vessels work along with the biceps and the triceps, the pectorals, the abdominals and the quadriceps, the life that pumps through the bone marrow is what keeps the body functioning.

Our muscles and blood vessels have a rhythm and a flow to maintain. They must obey the heart's direction to flow from all arteries including the brain. This keeps the body in harmony and on one accord. It keeps a generous and *continuous flow*. So as we offer our bodies in movement and praise unto the Lord, there is a special hormonal release that engulfs our entire being—this hormonal release is the *essence* of JOY!

The most diabolical attack for the sacred dancer happens in two areas: the mind and the **body.** When we are sick, we are weak. We stay in bed, our appetites are low, and our minds are not functioning at full capacity. When we are weak, many of our natural defenses are down—our immune system is very vulnerable at this stage. But it's not simply our physical immune system that's at stake, but our spiritual immune system as well. Satan's assignment is to rob us of our JOY. He is absolutely aware that there is a unique and supernatural grace upon the sacred dancer not only to maintain inner peace and joy, but also to EXUDE joy to God's people. This inner peace is found most frequently through making a direct connection between our spirit and the Spirit of God. Some may refer to it as *prayer.* In the life of the Believing sacred dancer, one comes to realize that our dances are as prayers, having the power to evoke the physical and emotional healing necessary to maintain the joy of the Lord. This is a *moving faith*, which brings about joy that one must refuse to allow the devil to steal!

During a meeting of the American Academy of Family Physicians in 1996, out of 296 physicians surveyed, 99% were convinced that the religious beliefs of their patients could heal them. Furthermore, 75% believed that the *prayers of others* could promote a patient's recovery. (Benson, H. "Timeless Healing", New York: Fireside, 1996) As ministers of dance, we have the awesome opportunity to dance the prayers of others until their healing comes and their joy is restored!

It is essential that sacred dancers live a life of consecration and holiness unto the Lord. However, the key to this consecration is a love-offering full of Joy. This joy is not weak, silly, or phony. This joy requires little or no effort. Why? Because it is our LIFE SOURCE! Our LIFE LINE. This is the sacred dancer's entry into His healing presence— When the King of Kings extends His royal scepter and beckons us to come. We "will" ourselves to enter His gates with thanksgiving, and come into His courts with praise. We must be the true worshippers of the Most High. As familiar as it may sound, it is an absolute Truth. This is the dancer's FULLNESS of joy. If we do not maintain health and complete wholeness of the mind, body, and spirit, with consistent, conscious, and intentional exercise of the body temple, we shall surely die! When the Church truly embraces the pure, God-ordained meaning and purpose of what it means to 'rejoice', the face of worship in our local churches will change radically. How many Psalms, scriptures, and **songs** do we sing daily that implore us to "Rejoice!", but instead we very dryly and lifelessly clap our hands and barely sway to the melody? This is wrong! If you or your church continue to perpetuate the idea that all of these 'extraneous' movements are unnecessary, not biblical, and worldly, consider the following scripture:

> **"Jesus replied, I saw satan fall like lightning from heaven. I have given you authority to trample on snakes and scorpions and to overcome all the power of the enemy; nothing will harm you. However, do not rejoice that the spirits submit to you, but rejoice that your names are written in the Book of Life. At that time,** *Jesus rejoiced in the Holy Spirit and praised His Father, Lord of Heaven..."*
> **Luke 10:21**

Our Dancing Savior

Jesus DANCED! He was not bound by public opinion or tradition. Nor did He believe that His public display of leaping, jumping, and whirling about would threaten His masculinity. Jesus danced! He was free and liberated in His Spirit, and the Father would have us to be the same. 2Cor. 3:17-18 tells us that "Where the Spirit of the Lord is, there is liberty. And now, we, who with unveiled faces all reflect the Lord's glory, are being transformed into His likeness with ever-increasing glory, which comes from the Lord who is the Spirit." If we are to be TRANSFORMED into His likeness we must break free from the borders and boundaries that keep us locked in our own tiny worlds of what we have known as 'praise'. In the breaking free, you will discover a new dimension in God.

Why Do We Rejoice?

We have many reasons to rejoice. First and foremost, it is

41

a command from the throne of God. As we rejoice as the scriptures say, we supernaturally baptize ourselves IN God's love and joy! You become free to apply the joy as a HEALING agent. If you are reading this book and the devil has been trying to rob you of your JOY and your STRENGTH, in the name of the Lord Jesus Christ, rise to your feet and REJOICE! Let the sound of rejoicing come alive in you as you allow these declarations and meditations to free your spirit and liberate your thoughts:

REASONS and COMMANDS to REJOICE:

I WILL REJOICE in every GOOD THING!	**Deut. 26:11**
I WILL REJOICE in the presence of the LORD MY GOD!	**Deut. 16:11, 27:7**
I REJOICE in MY Salvation!	**1Sam. 2:1**
I REJOICE that MY NAME is written in the Book of LIFE!	**Luke 10:21**
As I SEEK HIM I WILL REJOICE and be GLAD!	**1Chr. 16:10**
I REJOICE because He has been SO MERCIFUL to ME!	**Psalm 32:11**
I REJOICE in the TRIUMPH of the Lord!	**Isa. 13:3**
I MUST REJOICE as a Daughter of ZION!	**Zeph. 3:14**

**I WILL REJOICE in
MY TRIBULATIONS!**   **Rom. 5:3**

**I REJOICE in MY
TESTIMONY!**   **1Cor. 1:12**

Revelation:
**I must rejoice and be exceedingly glad on my journey
to Transformation.**

These declarations bring Life to the Sacred Dancer's bones. Psalm 23:5 says that the Lord prepares a table for us in the presence of our enemies. Similarly, the Lord will cause us to *dance* in the presence of our enemies in order to demonstrate the power, dominion, and authority of His glory! As we glorify Him in movement—rejoicing in the Lord in times of praise, worship, and warfare, we unleash a comprehensive attack on satan and undo the evil works that he had in store for us. When the dancer ACTIVELY CHOOSES to put satan under his or her FEET, this shakes and shatters the walls of Hell!

Oh, how freeing it is to know that our joy is God's *"SECRET WEAPON"*! This knowledge must empower all sacred dance ministers to make their rejoicing **dangerously explosive!**

Prayer Declaration:

Father in the Name of Jesus, I stand poised to receive a LIFTING of my burdens;
I bring myself to you naked and unashamed; Thank you for creating me fearfully and wonderfully before the foundations of the earth; God, thank you for my BODY-TEMPLE which I present to you today;
Thank you for cleansing me in my innermost parts; I release NOW all condemnation, guilt, and shame for the sins committed in this broken vessel; Thank you that right now, in the Name of Jesus, I supernaturally RECLAIM every part of myself that was given away, stripped away, or taken away at the hand of the enemy AND in my ignorance; I RECEIVE and EMBRACE the True JOY that you have for me, Lord; Impart in me now the very ESSENCE of joy so that I may rejoice together in Wholeness and Victory for the sake of your Kingdom, In the Name of the Father, the Son, and the Holy Spirit, AMEN.

Reader's Reflections:

(Fill in your own personal statements of affirmation.)

My Affirmations:

I Believe _____

_____

_____

I Release _____

_____

_____

I Declare _____

_____

_____

Sacred AFFIRMATION #3:

I AM Called to Commune with God through Dance!
I BELIEVE that God's Heart Yearns for Believers to Dance Unto Him!
I KNOW that I Will See All Nations Worship the Living God in Dance!
I DESIRE Complete and Total Liberation through Sacred Dance in the Church Universal!

CHAPTER THREE

What Is Liturgical Dance?

"Blessed is the one who finds wisdom, the one who gains understanding, for she is more profitable than silver and yields better returns than gold." Proverbs 3:13-14

In the development and establishment of the dance ministry in the Church today, there are several names and categories in which groups have placed themselves. Some familiar names are praise dancers, worship dancers, sacred dancers, dance choirs, dance chorales, Davidic dancers, and dance dramatists.

However, when one distinguishes him or herself as a *liturgical dancer*, there becomes a deeper accountability to God with regards to the ministry the individual intends to bring forth.

The word, 'liturgical' comes from the root word, 'liturgy'. A liturgy is defined as a 'eucharistic rite'. We are familiar with the word, 'Eucharist', as this is what the Early Church referred to when they spoke of the 'host' or the consecrated bread partaken of during the sacrament of Holy Communion.

A 'rite' is defined as that which is ceremonial in nature. It is done as a public, congregational, or community display of celebration. For example, in both the Jewish and African cultures, traditionally there is a grand observance of the ceremony known as Rites of Passage. It is at this ceremony where young boys and girls are celebrated as moving from one stage of life, childhood, to another, early adulthood. For the Jews, this is formally called a 'bar mitzvah' for males, and a 'bat mitzvah' for females. In any case, a rite, when practiced by the born-again Believer, is done specifically as an act of dedication and worship unto God.

Therefore, a Liturgical Dancer is one who expresses his or her faith through movement ministry in a public worship setting. The result and goal of this form of expression is *spiritual communion with God.*

Once individuals have declared themselves as such, the standard is raised in areas such as personal lifestyle, anointing, as well as the content and quality of the dance, which is brought before the Father and His people. This is also what distinguishes the **dancer** from the dance **ministry**. We are all dancers. We express ourselves in movement everyday and this has been going on since the beginning of time. The gift of dance was granted to us by God for many reasons—among them are thanksgiving and worship unto Him. So, truly, we are ALL called to dance! However, we are not all called to liturgical dance ministry. As this truth is more widely addressed and accepted, the Church will be free to explore even broader dimensions of worship and praise because each 'worshipper' will be positioned accordingly.

> ## Revelation:
> It is impossible to experience true worship and praise
> without relating it to an action of movement IN the
> body. We are ALL called to Dance
> before the Lord!

Biblical Foundations of Dance

While many individuals view dance done in the worship
setting as a new phenomenon, others are keenly aware that
dance is found throughout the Bible. In fact, one can find
references to movement and dance as far back as Genesis
1:1-3:

> **"In the beginning, God created the heavens
> and the earth. Now the earth was formless and
> empty, darkness was over the surface of the
> deep, and the Spirit of God was hovering over
> the waters. And God said, "Let there be light,"
> and there was light. "**

Verse two says that the Spirit of God *"hovered"* over the
waters. To hover is to stretch out, in an attitude of covering,
while slowly rocking or moving side to side or forward and
back. From the very beginning, movement was important to
God—so much so that He Himself danced as He created and
formed the Universe!

In studying the biblical uses and mentions of dance, one
will find over 25 occurrences of the English word 'dance',
and over 50 occurrences of Hebrew and Greek words in reference to an act or action that may be viewed as dance. The
liturgical dancer must understand the biblical and historical
origin of dance, as well as the significance of the movements
themselves. In this discovery, God will reveal the power and
purpose He has always had for dance to stir up joy, deliver-

ance, healing, warfare and worship. The following is not meant to be an exhaustive listing of the biblical references for dance, but will prove to be a steady indicator of the presence of dance and movement throughout the Holy Scriptures:

Dance as a Sign of Victory:

When Pharaoh's horses, chariots, and horsemen went into the sea, the Lord brought the waters of the sea back over them, but the Israelites walked through on dry ground. Then Miriam the prophetess, Aaron's sister, took a tambourine in her hand, and all the women followed her with tambourines and dancing.

(Exodus 15:19-20)

When the men were returning home after David had killed Goliath the Philistine, the women came out from all the towns of Israel to meet King Saul with singing and dancing, with joyful songs and with tambourines and lutes. As they danced, they sang: "Saul has slain his thousands and David his tens of thousands."

(1Samuel 18:6-7)

Dance As Restoration

The Lord appeared to us saying, "I have loved you with an everlasting love; I have drawn you with loving-kindness. I will build you up again and you will be rebuilt, O Virgin Israel. Again you will take up your tambourines and go out to dance with the joyful..."

(Jeremiah 31:3-4)

Dance As Celebration and Praise

They will be like a well-watered garden, and they will sorrow no more. Then maidens will dance and be glad, young men and old as well.

(Jeremiah 31:13)

While the girls of Shiloh were dancing at the annual feast of the Lord, each man caught one and carried her off to be his wife. Then they returned to their inheritance and rebuilt the towns and settled in them.

(Judges 21:23)

David, wearing a linen ephod, danced before the Lord with all his might, while he and the entire house of Israel brought up the ark of the Lord with shouts and the sound of trumpets.

(2Samuel 6:14)

Let's have a feast and celebrate! For this son of mine was dead and is alive again; he was lost and is found. So they began to celebrate. Meanwhile, the older son was in the field. When he came near, he heard music and dancing.

(Luke 15:23-25)

Dancing to Bring About Deliverance

Hear me, O Lord, and be merciful to me; O Lord be my help. You turned my mourning into dancing; you removed the sackcloth and clothed me with joy, that my heart may sing to you and not be silent.

(Psalm 30:10-12)

...A time to weep and a time to laugh; a time to mourn and a time to dance...

(Ecclesiastes 3:4)

Dance... Because God Likes It!

Let Israel rejoice in him that made him: let the children of Zion be joyful in their King. Let them praise his name in the dance and let them sing praises unto him with the timbrel and harp. For the Lord takes pleasure in his people; he will beautify the meek with salvation. *Let the saints be joyful in glory and let them give loud praises upon their beds.*

(Psalm 149:2-5)

Dance As Warfare

Thus saith the Lord: Clap with your hands and stamp with your feet, and say, "Alas for all the evil abominations of the house of Israel"!

(Ezekiel 6:11)

"Swords at the ready! Thrust right! Set your blade! Thrust left—wherever your edge is ordered! And I also will beat My fists together, and I will cause My fury to rest; I, the Lord, have spoken."

(Ezekiel 21:16-17)

"On the seventh day, they got up at daybreak and marched around the city seven times in the same manner, except that on that day they circled the city seven times. The seventh time around, when the priests sounded the trumpet blast, Joshua commanded the people, 'Shout! For the LORD has given you the city!'"

(Joshua 6:15-16)

Most Believers know that the original translation of the Bible was not written in English, rather it was written in Hebrew and Greek. It is because of this fact that the sacred dance minister finds his or her relevance and place within the Holy Scriptures, thus within the Church.

For the seasoned dance minister, these truths may serve as a simple point of review. However, there are many pastors, ministers, and laypersons that remain unaware of the power and anointing to be discovered in the application of sacred dance to their Worship Ceremonies and their daily lives. As the Scriptures remind us, we perish for lack of knowledge. But, we will also perish if we choose to sit on that knowledge and not activate it in the ways God intended for it to be utilized. On-going debates that squabble over doctrine, etiquette, methodology, and overall doubt concerning the effectiveness of sacred dance and the Arts as a vital tool for evangelism must come to a screeching halt! The doors must be opened to practical teaching and demonstration of these biblical truths regarding dance within our congregations, our cities, and our nations.

In our continuing desire to hear the prophetic voice of the Holy Spirit, we must also realize that God has already provided everything we need in order to be radically transformed in the ways in which we approach and experience "church". We must examine praise, worship, and warfare according to what the Spirit is doing now, and where the Spirit is leading us far into the 21st century. What is the provision already given to us by the Father? We need look no further than a full-length mirror to find the answer—OUR BODIES are the Lord's most exquisite instrument of change, and the Father longs to 'play' us as a sweet sounding melody to the Nations!

In the mirror, we see the manifestation of the Lord's own dream and vision. We see His answer to whom He desires to use in order to capture, save, and sanctify the souls of lost and wounded children. We see His answer to whom He wants to train and equip as warrior men and women who strategize with quiet confidence, but are never afraid to let out a "Ruwa!" (Hebrew word—loud aggressive cry of praise or victory in battle) shout against the enemies advances.

Sacred dance and movement during times of worship is one pathway to the Kingdom coming on earth. The fire and energy of the Holy Spirit is the *sanctifying* property. Our tears shed during times of worship provide a continual *cleansing*. The remembrance and acknowledgement of our own personal adversities that the Father has brought us through provides the *strengthening* agent. And our complete, sincere, and total abandonment in His presence brings forth *deliverance*. Now, when all of these things are working together, THIS is Victory!

There are at least 12 observed acts of **praise** *leading into* the act of **worship**. Of the 12, half of these acts are related to an *action of the body* through dance or movement. It is vital for us to combine the biblical origin and interpretation of Godly dance/movement expressions, with divine revelation of God's purpose and intent of the movements themselves. For this reason, an entire section of this book has been dedicated to a selective, yet detailed and instructional teaching on this topic. (**See *Appendix 1, Hebraic Movement Word- Study and Commentary*)**. This will prove to be vital information for the teacher of liturgical dance and the layperson alike. Each will discover that in addition to the English transliteration of the word, 'dance' as previously cited, there are many simple aspects of our everyday worship experience that are defined as movement and dance unto the Lord.

Proverbs 20:15 reminds us that the lips of knowledge are as precious jewels. Those who are called to the ministry of sacred artistry position themselves as jewels to the Kingdom, that is, the King Himself finds worth, pleasure and value in you! Thus, the dance minister should possess the ability to articulate, as well as have the appropriate understanding of the history, purpose, motive, and implications of every movement executed by their Body-Temples in ministry unto the Lord.

Prayer Declaration:

Dear Lord,
I give myself over to further study, meditation, education, and revelation concerning the Past, Present, and Kingdom-Future of purpose-filled movement!
You have given me the activity of my limbs in order to accomplish Your perfect will for the Kingdom.
I free my mind from all that I thought I knew, in exchange for All that You desire for me to KNOW.
I receive it now and fully intend to apply that which You have carefully sifted and assigned to me.
In Jesus' Name,
Amen.

Reader's Reflections:

(Fill in your own personal statements of affirmation.)

My Affirmations:

I Believe _____

_____

_____

I Confront _____

_____

_____

I Will_____

_____

_____

Sacred AFFIRMATION #4:

**I WILL Press My Heart Towards the Nations!
MY Nation Is the Head and NOT the Tail Through
JESUS CHRIST!
I AM A Messenger Called to PREPARE the WAY!
I MUST Become A Manifestation of God's Glory In the
Earth!**

CHAPTER FOUR

Discipling Nations and Transforming Households Through Sacred Artistry

"All the nations you have made will come and worship before you, O Lord; they will bring glory to your name. For you are great and do marvelous deeds." Psalm 89:6

How does one transform a nation? One does not. The African proverb that says, "It takes a *whole* village to raise a child" is usually read and interpreted to mean that it takes everyone to assist in the successful rearing of a child. However, in the context of transforming and healing nations, one should consider that a "whole" village is made up of men, women, boys, and girls who are healed completely in their minds, body, and spirits. They are "whole" individuals. Living and traveling among different cultures, one becomes painfully aware that this world is filled with wounded, violent, dejected, underprivileged, and virtually forgotten individuals. I have seen 1st-hand the faces of those in prisons and youth correctional facilities from the U.S. to Russia, from Africa and across the Caribbean. They are the faces of people who were in the wrong place at the wrong time, lost their tempers, and "accidentally" took someone's life. Sometimes, they are the faces of people who have suffered from a traumatic experience and have literally lost their minds. Now, their dreams are gone.

What always fascinates me is that some of these same individuals are the ones who are so brilliantly and naturally gifted in the Arts. It's as if satan specifically strategized to ruin their lives because of the gifting inside of them. These people are waiting for something—anything that can restore hope and bring joy to their dark circumstances. We as sacred artists have the unique opportunity to bring life and light to their dark circumstances. While people are wasting their lives away and others are becoming victims of unprecedented violence and murders, the sacred artists have the opportunity to minister restoration and healing to those who desperately need it.

Transformation and Discipleship

In the transformation process, discipleship is the primary tool. A nation in need of discipleship must start with a recognition of the past, that is, who we are and where we've come from, and how intricately we are woven into God's purpose and plan for His Kingdom. One key component to understanding our true heritage as anointed artists and Believers are the Biblical promises of God to us from generation to generation, accompanied with the cultural uniqueness of individual nations.

As this revelation is opened to us, we will begin to disciple one another as God intended. This is not to 'evangelize the heathen' (so-called), or witness for the purpose of perpetuating a slave mentality. By this, I'm referring to early, well-intentioned missionaries who brought the Gospel to many Third World nations, but after winning souls, neglected to continue in teaching valuable kingdom principles.

Among them include biblical teaching on tithing, faith, prosperity, healing, intercession, and the power of dance as an instrument of worship and praise to Jehovah God. While many accepted Christ as Savior, they later became corrupt in their morals and lifestyle values. Even though God honors the salvation decision and the attempt at righteous living, He will still render judgment on the wicked, perverse, and back-slidden.

As a result, many nations have been deprived of the awesome blessings that come with adherence to these and other biblical practices that were established by God in order to bring blessings to His people and their seed. Today, these effects are clearly manifested in that many of God's generational promises appear to have been exchanged for man's traditionalism, staunch ritualism, and piety within our churches.

If we are to reclaim the promises of God for this generation and generations to come, we must first begin in our own homes.

Praise that Transforms the Household

One such example of God's promise to bless generations as a result of their praise can be found in IISamuel 6:10. Here we find King David and his chosen men of Israel preparing to bring the Ark of God into the city of David in Jerusalem. In the midst of celebrating while carrying the Ark on a cart, the oxen stumbled, causing the Ark to fall. When one of David's men, Uzzah, reached out to catch it, the Lord God reacted strongly. While Uzzah's action was noble, it was also in direct violation of the law of God—that only authorized and anointed Levites must handle the Ark. Therefore, the Lord struck down Uzzah in death that day. Obedience is ALWAYS better than sacrifice—even in our praise! In Uzzah's zeal to participate in celebration, he seemingly lost sight of God's law.

As the scriptures continue, King David became angry and afraid of the Lord. He even became afraid of having this sacred Ark come into his city. He said in IISamuel 6:9, "How can the Ark of the Lord ever come to me?" King David was no longer willing to take the Ark with him. Instead, he ordered that the Ark be delivered to the house of a faithful Levite and servant of the Lord by the name of Obed-Edom.

Obed-Edom and his family were Gittites from an area called Gath, believed to be in the region of North Central Africa. And the Bible says in IISamuel 6:11-12:

"The Ark of God remained in the house of Obed-Edom the Gittite for three months, and the Lord blessed him and his entire household. Now King David was told, "The Lord has blessed the household of Obed-Edom and everything he has because of the Ark of God".

What happened in the life of Obed-Edom and his family during those three months? While the Bible does not offer a specific, detailed account, there are a few key observations that can be made. The Ark of God represented the actual presence of the Lord.

We also know that God inhabits or dwells within the praises of His people. In order for God's blessings to rest abundantly upon the entire household of Obed-Edom, a significant amount of true worship and praise must have been present. More importantly, it must have been *pleasing* to Jehovah God. It is interesting to note that while Obed-Edom was indeed a Levitical servant of the Most High God, he was also of African descent. Therefore, his style of worship and praise to God would have been unique to his culture. One could only imagine how Obed-Edom must have led his family in daily devotions to God through a powerful combination of exuberant, zealous praise in song, traditional dance, and prayer. It's no wonder that God promised, and did in fact bless his entire household and everything he had!

This blessing was so powerful that King David himself had to experience what God was doing. So after three months, his fear subsided and he went to Obed-Edom's home to collect the Ark. Again, the Bible does not say specifically what kind of conversation was had between King David and Obed-Edom as the Ark was turned over. However, as a servant of the Lord, and as a man who is accountable to King David, Obed-Edom must have given the King a full report of what took place over the past three months.

I wonder if Obed-Edom may have said to King David something like this: "Oh King David! How excellent is the Name of the Lord! He has blessed everything I have. Do you know what I have discovered? I believe that Jehovah God delights in my family's praises to Him! It was as if the Spirit of God was stirring within my home. And do you know what else? His presence is felt even *stronger* when we dance before Him! I believe He actually *enjoys* our rejoicing! May I suggest, my King, you should try it as well!"

It is not surprising that as the story continues, we see King David for what the world now makes him famous for in IISamuel 6:12-15:

> "...so **David went down and brought up the Ark of God from the house of Obed-Edom to the City of David with <u>rejoicing</u>. When those who were carrying the Ark of the Lord had taken six steps, he sacrificed a bull and a fattened calf. David, wearing a linen ephod, danced before the Lord with all his might, while he and the entire house of Israel brought up the Ark of the Lord with shouts and the sound of trumpets."**

What an exciting time for King David and the people of Israel! At no other time in history had the people ever seen a King do a dance that was holy unto the Lord God Jehovah! This was what became so powerful, and liberating. It was not the fact that a man danced, however, it was that this man was a King and that he danced with such abandon before the Lord.

During every transformation or change in a nation, the people of that nation are watching their leaders. The same is true for the Church. The people in the congregation watch the actions and the spirit of their Pastors and leadership to decide whether or not they will support or reject something. For a nation, the decision may be political, and the views of the Prime Minister or President will determine how individuals will vote. People are looking for someone with passion and vision to lead them to a better way of living, a better emotional state, and a richer, deeper spiritual life. As it was with King David, the *entire house* of Israel followed him in praise. They followed King David because not only did he have a personal vision of himself in celebratory worship to God, but he extended his vision of corporate celebration throughout Israel.

It was immediately following this act of celebration that a spirit of jealousy and condemnation confronted the King through his wife Michal. David's response is what we, as sacred artists and dance ministers, must hold on to as part of our heritage. The King said:

> **"It was before the Lord, who chose me rather than your father or anyone from his house when he appointed me ruler of the Lord's people Israel—I will celebrate before the Lord. I will become even more undignified than this, and I will be humiliated in my own eyes. But by those whom you've spoken of, I will be held in honor." IISamuel 6:21**

In every artistic demonstration, it must be clear in one's heart, mind, and spirit that what is executed is done, "before the Lord". If this is not settled, the enemy will succeed in his attempts to undermine and sabotage our ministries by allowing the opinions of men and women to dictate the frequency, venue, intensity and direction in which our ministries are fully experienced. Sometimes, the opinions of man will serve as a tactic of the enemy to minimize the impact in which your demonstrated praise had with on-lookers. Receiving this as truth would be death to the sacred artist's success in future ministry. Furthermore, it would greatly hinder our inspiration to become what the world may view as "even more undignified" in the presence of the Lord. Today's Church needs Pastors and leaders with the same quality of confidence, conviction, and discernment regarding dance in their congregations. They must be willing and able to distinguish between true spiritual praise, versus utter foolishness and displays of the flesh. This will allow the leaders to feel free to encourage congregational acceptance and participation in this vital form of praise.

King David's stern response to his wife's objections, accompanied with his previous display of praise captured the heart of God so much so that He made the following promises to him:

> **"...This is what the Lord Almighty says: 'I will make your name great, like the names of the greatest men of the earth. And I will provide a place for my people Israel and will plant them so that they can have a home of their own and no longer be disturbed. Wicked people will not oppress them anymore, as they did at the beginning and have done ever since the time I appointed leaders over my people Israel. I will also give you rest from all of your enemies. The**

Lord declares to you that the Lord himself will establish a house for you: When your days are over, and you rest with your father, I will raise up your offspring to succeed you; I will establish his kingdom. He is the one who will build a house for my Name and I will establish the throne of his kingdom forever. I will be his father, and he will be my son. When he does wrong, I will punish him with the rod of men. But my love will never be taken away from him, as I took it away from Saul, whom I removed from before you. Your house and your kingdom will endure forever before me; your throne will be established forever.' " IISamuel 7:8-16

The same promises made to the household of Obed-Edom, King David, and the house of Israel can be received for our own households and our nations today if we are willing to be obedient, sacrificial, and sincere in our motives and expressions of praise and worship offered to the Lord. God is vitally concerned with our households. The household can either be our homes, our churches, our communities, or our nations—it depends on how broad your vision is! The question is, how can we extend our vision of corporate, celebratory worship to the Lord as a way to transform our households, nations, and the world?

Consider the following steps that may serve as introductory principles to assist in the transformation process:

STEPS TO TRANSFORMING YOUR HOUSEHOLD:
1. **Radical Aggression in Personal Prayer and Intercession**: We must seek the face of God and pray the Word concerning our family—in particular those unsaved family members and those who are not living

a godly lifestyle. Become violent in your prayers that call down the fire from heaven upon their lives until they totally surrender to the Lord Jesus Christ, repent, and live a lifestyle worthy of their calling. Caution: these prayers may be dangerous as the point is to win your loved one's lost soul **by any means** necessary. Always call forth the absolute perfect will of God concerning your loved one's life. As you pray, call forth the 'Zoë' or the 'God kind of life' on the inside of them. Call forth the purpose for their lives as God did in Jeremiah 1:5. Concerning your nation—seek the face of God and pray the Word concerning your leaders, heads of state, government officials, and pastors. There will be serious spiritual strongholds in this arena, which can only be destroyed through the offering of a pure sacrifice. Therefore, cleanse your heart completely when praying for your nation. Ask for revelation, discovery into the unknown systems of the world, and wisdom to know and understand clearly what should be done. Pray consistently for Holy Spirit-filled Believers with integrity to take their rightful positions in leading our nation. Also pray that your leaders receive the impartation of the spirit of praise—this was vital for King David, and it is for any leader. All true leaders should be worshippers. Your nation must experience freedom in every sense of the word if it is going to be used of God for His strategic positioning to be an example to other nations of His abundant blessings.

2. **Household Fasting:** Call for a time of fasting in your entire household. Your household may be whatever area in which you have direct supervision, authority, or dominion over. Initially, view your household as yourself—that is your own body. Then, your household may extend to every member of your family currently living

under your roof. Your family home may then extend to your business—especially if you are the owner or you have hired persons to work for you specifically. Is your entire household saved? This will make a big difference in how they respond to your call to fast. God wants to save individuals, households, and entire nations of people; however, we must take authority over our households and everything that takes place therein. If there is sin or any evil practices taking place in your household, it will be revealed during this time of consecration. During the fast, eliminate all music, television programming, book/magazine reading, or conversations that **do not give glory** and honor to God. Finally during your fast, practice a season of silence. While hard at first, this will prove to be a powerful instrument in hearing from God during your time of fasting.

3. **Corporate Worship Experience:** The corporate worship experience is indeed one of the tools and gifts provided by God in order to keep us built up in the faith. However, it is also something that is most taken for granted. After days or weeks of encountering stress, harassment, conflict, and all manner of obstacles, there is nothing like coming into the presence of the Lord with fellow Believers. In the book of Hebrews, the Word of God reminds us not to "forsake the assembly of the saints". This is not just to attend church as a form or fashion of tradition. Rather, church attendance should grow out of a desire to hear from the Lord. It should also grow out of an intense need to offer Him worship through every aspect of our lives—whether it is through praise, tithing, serving, encouraging the brethren, or prayer. Corporate church attendance must evolve into a corporate *worship experience!* The expectation is that something so wonderfully 'GOD' is going to happen, and you just can't afford to miss it!

4. **Speaking Prophetic Declarations:** When it comes to you and your house, God is expecting results. What does not get spoken does not come into being. In making prophetic declarations, we loan ourselves to the Holy Spirit in order to be propelled into the future supernaturally. We open ourselves to the will, plan, and purpose of the Father—that is, the things concerning **us.** With that glimpse, the Holy Spirit then zooms us back into the present where God awaits us to speak and proclaim the vision or revelation with authority, power, and conviction. For example, you may have been praying for salvation of your brother's soul for years without any physical manifestation. However, in the spirit realm, you SEE him saved and serving the Lord in many, many ways, you must begin to speak what you see, by faith! Stop sitting on your revelation and declare it in the earth as it is in heaven.

5. **Practice and Application of Dance Unto the Lord (Public and Private):** Dancing unto the Lord is an expression of praise and worship. We know that worship must be a lifestyle, which means it is something incorporated and woven into every aspect of our lives—not set apart for special occasions and the Sunday morning church experience. Regardless of our denominational background, the Word of God continuously admonishes us to "praise the Lord"; to "let everything that has breath praise the Lord"; to "rejoice in the Lord Always"; and to praise him with the tambourine and dance. I often wonder how a command from God, which is so straightforward, could get lost through the "interpretation" and traditionalism in many of our local churches. Some of these churches still refuse to embrace individual or congregational dancing in the church. There are those assemblies which allow 'dance', but see it only as a means to keep

the youth active, busy, and a part of things. It is evident that these pastors do not really embrace dance, therefore they are only spectators in the worship experience. Some sit by, watching stiffly as if enduring some unusual punishment. As displayed in the life of King David, the leader's response to worship will oftentimes govern the congregation's overall willingness to give themselves over to worship. God have mercy on us for stifling the move of the Holy Spirit due to our own personal bondages!

Our households are in need of deliverance and one pathway of deliverance can occur through public and private worship in dance unto God. As one allows the Holy Spirit to speak to us through the process outlined, one will begin to feel a shifting taking place on the inside. This shift is actually a dramatic, spiritual paradigm shift of perceptions, reasoning's, and motives. Gradually, the body will yield more and more to the will of the Father. It may begin in a public worship setting with a simple action of lifting the hands. Eventually the movement may incorporate a wave, a rocking, or a swaying. As we learn in our Hebrew word study of dance, there are specific movements/actions executed which carry specific power and anointing in the spiritual realm. Progressively, the Spirit of Liberation will take residence on the inside of one's spirit. This liberation may be from self-inflicted bondage, personal trials, addictions, unforgiveness—whatever the issue may be; when you are ready and willing to be set free at any expense, don't be surprised if your body begins to leap, jump, and whirl about!

The Psalmist even testifies to the delivering power of dance by declaring to God in Psalm 30:11, "You have turned for me my mourning into dancing; You've removed my sackcloth and clothed me with joy…"

Are you willing to bring this worship experience through

sacred dance into your home? As our families come together for morning devotions and prayer, we can incorporate praise and worship dance unto the Lord by simply putting on our favorite Christian CD and allow the Holy Spirit to minister and flow freely to us and within us. Remember, it is impossible to experience *true worship* without a bodily response. The household of Obed-Edom was blessed abundantly as a result of his obedience to worship and serve in God's presence. As we extend God's vision of abundant blessings for our household and apply these principles to our daily family living with fervent consistency, we will discover a new, fresh anointing and vision for worship that will bring salvation, deliverance, and freedom in expressing our adoration of God. Infuse your house—physically and spiritually, with total praise and your home will never be the same!

Praise that Transforms the Culture

The use of Sacred Arts is one way to encourage nations to celebrate and worship God in their own cultural context, while continuing to embrace the richness and heritage of others. One nation who is making this concept a reality is the beautiful island of Jamaica in the West Indies.

Historically, Jamaica has been known for its soulful and dynamic reggae rhythms. Whether nationally or internationally, Christian or non-Christian, most persons immediately associate reggae music with the late singer/musician Bob Marley. Much of what Marley wrote and sang about concerned social reformation of his country and the world. As a missionary to Jamaica over the past two years, I have come to understand that while Mr. Marley continues to be highly respected and honored as an international music legend, he can not be given credit for **creating** the reggae sound. A sound so rich could not have come forth from a mere mortal. Rather, the uniqueness of reggae music was a gift from God to the Nation, birthed out of the heart cries, souls, and spirits of a people in a never-ending quest for freedom, hope and justice. The powerful accomplishment of Bob Marley was that he took reggae music out of the Caribbean venue and into the world. However, what many persons outside of the Caribbean do not realize is that while many of his lyrics may be described as positive, redemptive, and empowering, they also promote the cult of Rastafarianism, which does not accept the Lordship of Jesus Christ.

Rastafarians also maintain many ancestral African traditions and practices. They have taken those traditions and have **added** things such as all-natural food intake, natural hair, dreadlocks, style of dance, drums, and the 'spiritual' engagement in smoking ganja—all of which have become associated with the Rastafarian culture. This has been one of the key setbacks as to why the majority of the churches in Jamaica do not embrace anything that sounds too reggae, or looks too 'African'.

Therefore, while Jamaica can indeed boast of her beauty and diversity, it is also a country of great psychological, spiritual, and physical need. In many ways, satan has been able to pervert the gift of reggae music from the Lord to the Jamaican people, and as a result, the perversion of the dances **to** this music has occurred.

However, over the past 10 years, amidst all of the political, social, and moral turmoil, God has begun to shake and stir the secular music world throughout the Caribbean. Many prominent secular singers, rap artists, and DJ's are giving their lives to Christ and taking the international gospel music world by storm. In particular, they are influencing the youth and young adults like never before. Now, they minister the Gospel through their art form with even more power and zeal as they did when they were in the world.

It's a fresh, aggressive anointing that is raising up individuals who are not afraid to engage in spiritual combat because they are confident that they will emerge victorious.

While the Church is still not fully receptive, this has indeed caught the attention of pastors, elders, and bishops who are being called upon to comment on this radical change for the Kingdom. Inevitably, once the musicians and singers get saved, the dancers must follow! Now what was previously known as reggae music has become the 'Kingdom Sound' of a nation. The singers and musicians possess the breath of God required to stir up the Spirit of the Dance that lies dormant in the bellies of thousands of potential worshippers!

The use of music, song, dance, drama, and the other sacred arts is indeed a way that God ordained, uses, and approves of to bring His Word to life for those non-Believers who may never step foot inside of a church. It is also a way for the world to hear the cry of a hurting people. For those who are Believers, the use of sacred arts is God's way of demonstrating the liberation and freedom He has freely given us in our bodies when the movement is done unto Him.

We must do everything we can to capture and take authority of the space and the territory that belongs to us in the natural and in the spirit realm. As we claim land for the Kingdom, we must also reclaim our own creative souls and minds as well. This will take a radical approach. For some, it may mean teaching gang members to dramatize real-life situations with Biblical principles. Or, it may mean teaching physically and sexually abused little girls to turn their mourning into dancing. Whatever it takes, those of us who are called to this area of ministry must be willing to take up the challenge for the sake of the next generation and the future of the Sacred Arts.

Our children are the ones who will be running the world in the next millennium. Therefore, a supernatural impartation must take place in the soul of every child we encounter. The seed must be planted for the advancement of the Kingdom. As ministers of the Arts, this is not the time for us to be selfish and self-centered on 'our ministries' only. It will take much love and discipleship in order for us to reclaim our sisters and brothers for Christ. With that love, we must snatch them out from ungodly activity in the dance-halls, nightclubs, strip joints, porno films, comedy clubs, demonic and seductive art forms, and music with lyrics and themes that are an abomination to God.

All of these things contribute to one's perception of their body, their self-respect, and self-esteem. Once the individual is reclaimed, we will reclaim the village. Once the village has been reclaimed, we can possess the nation for the Kingdom of God. Only then are we adequately qualified to extend ourselves to our neighboring nations with the message of healing and reconciliation through the universal language mediums of song, dance, drama, and joy.

Prayer Declaration:

Father, thank You for clarity, purpose and understanding;
I commit myself now to continuing to seek Your face
and studying
Your Word for fresh revelation; Lord let the words of my
mouth, the meditations of
My heart, and the motivation for the movements of my
body be pleasing,
Pure, and glorious in Your sight, now and throughout
Eternity; Help me to unselfishly teach and
Train an army of consecrated ministers—even my own
household, who can set the captives FREE!
In Jesus' Name,
AMEN.

Reader's Reflections:

(Fill in your own personal statements of affirmation.)

My Affirmations:

My household is filled with _____

_____

_____

My household must receive _____

_____

_____

My household shall be _____

_____

_____

Sacred AFFIRMATION #5

**I AM being molded into His image and likeness!
I HAVE the ability to LISTEN for His Voice!
I WILL NOT be distracted by a world full of Chaos!
I WILL NOT be INTIMIDATED by Stares and Glares!**

I MUST surrender to His Perfect Will.

CHAPTER 5:

In Christ, I Hear and Obey: HEARING THE CALL

"...And the Lord called Samuel again a third time. And he arose and went to Eli, and said Here am I, for thou didst call me. And Eli perceived that it was the LORD who had called the child. Therefore Eli said unto Samuel, Go lie down, and it shall be that if he calls unto you again, you will say: Speak Lord, for thy servant heareth. So Samuel went and lay down in his place. And the Lord came and stood, and called as at the other times saying, Samuel, Samuel! Then Samuel said, Speak Lord, for thy servant heareth..." 1Samuel 3:8-10

How does one identify a true call from the Lord? As it was with young Samuel, he was unsure about whom it was that called to him. In his youth, he was unable to distinguish the voice of the Lord from his master, Eli. He knew that he **heard someone,** but didn't know that it was the Lord. However, when the truth was revealed to him, he was able to clearly identify the Lord's voice for himself. He not only identified it, but he heard and obeyed the voice.

While some tradition may say that a call is held exclusively for the preaching ministry, God has always had a much broader view of the call that He places on an individual's life. For example, when the prophet Jeremiah received his initial call, the Bible says that the word of the Lord came to him saying, "Before I formed you in your mother's womb, I knew you. Before you were born, I consecrated you and appointed you a prophet to the nations..." Later, the Lord revealed His even greater plan of using Jeremiah as one of His key vessels to proclaim and execute judgment among Jerusalem. Just as God calls individuals, He also calls individual nations to fulfill a specific purpose in the earth. The problem is that when individuals refuse to obey the call of God on their lives, it results in an entire Nation of disobedient and corrupt individuals who sabotage their own deliverance. These nations are destined to suffer God's judgment and will potentially forfeit their chance to fulfill their potential. As Proverbs 1:24 says:

"Because I have called you, and you refused to listen; because I have stretched out my hand and no one has heeded; and because you have ignored all my counsel and would have none of my reproof, I also will laugh at your calamity; I will mock when panic strikes you. When panic strikes you like a storm, and your calamity comes like a whirlwind, when distress and anguish come upon you; then they will call upon me, but I will not answer; they will seek me diligently, but will not find me."

Many sacred dance ministers and worship artists are suffering right now as a result of pride and disobedience. This suffering may manifest itself as stunted growth in our personal ministries, turmoil in our personal lives, or even continuous conflict in circumstances around us which we are ignorantly labeling as 'warfare'. When one continues to ignore God's call to minister in the Arts, it has a tremendous ripple effect on all those who have been pre-destined to benefit and be blessed by what God has put inside of you. How many of our elderly will not receive healing in their bodies because you refuse to go to the hospitals and the nursing homes and dance under the anointing of the Holy Spirit? How many untimely deaths and imprisonment will steal countless numbers of our young boys because you neglected to nurture their gifts of music and song? How many little girls will be wooed over to secular entertainment, starring in ungodly music videos because you refused to train them in the sacred dance ministry as God directed? If one understands that obedience is better than sacrifice, then one's life depends on submission to the full measure of the call of God on one's life—we cannot pick and choose which parts of the call we will adhere to. Full measure means ALL.

More About The Call

A call speaks to a burden or a passion to do something or FOR something. The central focus of the Call of the Sacred Dancer is the deep desire and passion to see the souls of Nations saved AND lives changed through the power and anointing of the Sacred Dance. The next question that must be answered is concerning *specialization*. In other words, to what specific AREA of dance ministry have you been called to? In order to clarify the vision, we look at the structure and the *ministry gifts* that Jesus established for us:

> **"And He gave some apostles, and some, prophets; and some, evangelists; and some, pastors and teachers for the perfecting of the**

saints, for the work of the ministry, and for the edifying of the body of Christ; until we all come in the unity of the faith, and of the knowledge of the Son of God, unto a perfect man, unto the measure of the stature of the fullness of Christ..." Ephesians 4:11-13

The five-fold ministry is a term, which has become very familiar to Believers, yet is not always embraced in its entirety. Every person called to ministry works within this God-given framework initially. How can this be applied to the sacred dance minister? We may be dancers and worshippers, but we all have a different mission, purpose, and assignment given to us by God. Your job and mine is to find out what it is! Once the sacred dancer understands what *office* or ministry gift is being exercised in order to accomplish his or her particular mission, an 'inner-liberation' will occur. The individual is released to flow in their gift—not that which has been put upon them. For some, this realization will take a supernatural impartation of understanding from the Holy Spirit!

Unfortunately, our 'appearance' of dominion, authority, and confidence does not always carry over into our inner-spirits, our ministry, and our place in the church. It is possible that you will serve in a church with a Pastor who has not yet embraced this revelation and as a result, your physical body is not free to manifest your calling. This is why it is critical that WE KNOW our calling is sure. When we are sure of that which God has birthed us for, we become uniquely effective and precise in our approach. We become intentional in prayer and intercession for God's Will concerning us. Our times of intercession will increase for our pastors and those in authority over us. Rather than becoming rebellious and resentful, we put our energies to action in PRAYER and stay focused on His plan.

It could be that God has positioned you in a particular church for the very purpose of revolutionizing the worship experience through dance and sacred artistry! If this is your assignment, please know that God will equip, prepare, and give you grace for the journey. Also know that this assignment is **hard ground to breakthrough. S**ometimes God will allow us to come up against opposition and resistance in order to reveal a deeper spiritual truth. The truth may be that there is a demonic stronghold that has been operating within your church for many years. It could be that this is preventing the pastor or the congregation from receiving the very thing that will usher in the power and presence of the Holy Spirit in a way unfamiliar to them. In order for us to become strategists, specialists, and EXECUTIONERS in God's plan for sacred dance to the Church and the Nations, we must work solely within our own gifting and calling. This will serve as one of the best tactics against the enemy's attempt to sabotage our success.

Revelation:

There is something that only <u>you</u> can do for the Kingdom. The Lord is aware of it and He is now requiring that of you. You must work the works of Him who sent you while it is still day.

Identifying the Office of the Sacred Dance Minister

"I urge you, as a prisoner for the LORD, that you live a life worthy of the calling you have received. Be completely humble and gentle; be patient, bearing with one another in love. Make every effort to keep the unity of the Spirit through the bond of peace. There is one body

and one Spirit - just as you were called to one hope when you were called - one baptism; one God and Father of all who is over all, through all, and in all..." Ephesians 4:1-6

How can dance possibly be viewed in a similar manner as the five-fold ministry? While some may find this dispensation somewhat controversial, others will view it as perfectly natural and receive it in the spirit that it is stated. In applying the relevance of the five-fold ministry gifts to the sacred dance minister, we are able to clearly identify certain characteristics about the motivations, purpose, and intent of the dance ministries in which we are a part of. It will also clarify some specific choreographic styles and motivations for the dance minister individually. Several years ago, I asked one of my beloved mentors, Dr. Cecelia Williams Bryant, a question regarding which office of the 5-fold ministry she was called to. Her response was "Whichever one the Lord needs me to walk in at the appointed time". This response shaped the future of my philosophy about personal ministry. I discovered that I must be totally open to the Holy Spirit in allowing any and all gifts that God wanted to develop within me without restriction. However, I also discovered that as I yielded to God, He began to bring forth and identify my <u>dominant</u> gift. One's dominant gift is the one, above all else, which you are absolutely **compelled to do successfully.** Therefore, in the life of the dance minister, it is important to see yourself as a 'specialist' in your dominant area of gifting. In all of this, we remind ourselves that with the many different gifts and callings, their is only one Spirit and one God who is the Father, Owner, and Giver of ALL the gifts.

<u>The Apostolic Dancer</u>
The first ministry gift of the Church is that of the Apostle. These are those who are sent and assigned by God with the

task of starting and overseeing churches. Thus, the apostolic dancer is viewed as one who is "sent forth". The apostolic dancer must have a broad, global vision of their calling to all the world. An apostolic calling on the dancer's life signifies those persons specifically chosen by the Lord for a particularly special training, or mission. These dancers will have ministry gifts and callings which cause them to birth new and unique dance ministries across the world, while serving as a spiritual guide to the leaders of those ministries. Some characteristics of a dance minister who may have an apostolic ministry calling on his or her life are:

- Nations-minded
- Trains leaders and has a true heart for leaders
- Disciplined in his/her personal affairs
- Operates according to protocol, order, and consideration of impact to others
- Anointed with supernatural wisdom and keen insight to discern the motives of others
- Skilled in conflict-resolution and reconciliation as it relates to individuals and/or groups
- Excellent management skills

The Prophetic Dancer

A prophet is one who boldly speaks forth and openly proclaims divine messages or revelations from the Lord. These messages come by way of the Holy Spirit and may manifest through dreams, visions, word of knowledge, word of wisdom, interpretation of tongues or some other unction of the Holy Spirit. Thus, the prophetic dancer is one anointed to bring forth and openly proclaim these same messages with their BODY. He or she is one who is able to interpret the Word of God through movement spontaneously given to them as the Holy Spirit gives utterance. In keeping with 1Corinthians 14:1-3, dances that come forth from the prophetic dancer will comfort, strengthen, or encourage the

Church. Some characteristics of a dance minister who may have a prophetic ministry calling on their lives may be:
- He or she is an intercessor
- Possesses supernatural gifts of discernment, interpretation of tongues, and interpretation of dreams
- Will move/act very spontaneously according to the leading of the Holy Spirit
- Actively engages himself or herself in spiritual warfare through dance
- Has a strong sense of integrity/truth in personal affairs and in movement interpretation
- Carries an anointing to pull down strongholds and bring about deliverance in spoken word or dance

The Dance Evangelist

An Evangelist is one whose primary ministry purpose is evangelical in nature. That is, the evangelist has a deep burden and desire to bring lost souls to Jesus Christ. The Dance Evangelist will always seek to manifest the fact that, "God so loved the World that He gave His only begotten Son, and whosoever would believe in Him shall not perish, but have everlasting life...", (John 3:16). Therefore, the Dance Evangelist will strive to minister in a way that convinces and convicts persons of their sins, thus bringing them to repentance. Some characteristics of the dance minister who may have an evangelistic ministry may be:
- Has an unusual burden to travel throughout the world
- Very radical and innovative in their approach to soul winning
- Strong compassion for the poor and underprivileged
- Called to minister outside the church, i.e. prison, street, hospital ministry appeals to him/her
- Anointed to bring persons to repentance through his or her ministry
- Possesses the ability to travail in their dance until a

breakthrough occurs

The Dance Pastor and Teacher

A Pastor is one who is responsible for overseeing the spiritual welfare of Believers. A Pastor must also have the ability and anointing of a Teacher. Teachers are those who have special gifts and abilities to teach, explain, and expound on the Word of God. For the Dance Pastor and Teacher, this is done through a variety of ways, but primarily through discipleship, teaching, and accountability. The Dance Pastor and Teacher understands the importance of living a holy and consecrated life unto the Lord. These are usually the leaders or directors of Sacred Dance Ministries. These persons are responsible for identifying, discerning, and nurturing the spiritual growth of their dancers based on their observations and inter-actions with their members. These observations may occur through group prayer and devotional time, group Bible study, church attendance, and the level of anointing operating in that person's dance ministry overall. Therefore, the Dance Pastor and Teacher must LIVE a lifestyle that is worthy of their calling. The Dance Pastor and Teacher is one who is willing to open themselves up to the scrutiny of the masses as a result of a deep, sincere compassion for the well-being of God's people. Some characteristics of a dance minister who may have a teaching/pastoral ministry calling are:
- Possesses the heart of a servant
- Sincere compassion and love for people
- Called to teach children and youth; does so effectively and joyously
- Possesses the heart of a shepherd
- Supernatural wisdom and keen discernment of the needs of people
- Anointed with a 'magnetic' personality
- Extremely organized and detail-oriented

Revelation:
The power of knowing who you are lies in the knowledge that your destination is Success.

Prayer Declaration:

Dear Lord,
Thank you, Lord for being patient with me. I understand now that I have been called, taken, blessed, chosen, and broken to be given to humanity as a shining example of the love, power, compassion, and glory of You and Your Son Jesus Christ. Help me now, Father, to fulfill all that you have called me to do. Forgive me for not walking in the Light that you purposed me to walk in. I understand now that my obedience must be unto you in ALL things;
I surrender my passions and desires to you
to form and shape them;
I trust you Father to only put the desires, gifts, and callings in my heart that You want. Here I am.
Change Me, Lord!
In Jesus' Name,
AMEN.

Reader's Reflections:

(Fill in your own personal statements of affirmation.)

My Affirmations:

My dominant gift is _____

_____

_____

I recognize that I must _____

_____

_____

I will not force _____

_____

_____

Sacred AFFIRMATION #6

I AM Called to Obedience in Christ!
I CAN LIVE Holy!
I WILL Glorify God with My Whole Body!
I HAVE the Keys to the Kingdom!
I MUST Consecrate My Mind, Body, and Spirit DAILY
I BELIEVE God!

CHAPTER 6

Triumph in the Battle for
DISCIPLINE

One of the most effective strategies of satan concerning God's chosen vessels is the manipulation of the sacred dancer's mind. We have already identified the sacred dancer as 'God's secret weapon' in spiritual warfare. Because of this, our desire to engage in warfare is NOT OPTIONAL. We will participate, whether willingly or kicking and screaming—literally. Therefore, it is here, in the mind that the first conflict begins. When Jesus was crucified, it was at a location called 'Golgotha', which means 'the place of the skull'. For the sacred dance minister, this is the territory most difficult to conquer. A virtual breeding ground for unyielded desires, thoughts, and habits. It is also where we must learn to develop and strengthen the power our minds have over the flesh.

We should realize that the greater the depth and breadth of the dancer's revelation from God is, the more VIOLENT, blatant and devastating are the assaults from satan. Please don't take this lightly. God's chosen vessels in the area of the Sacred and Performing Arts are TARGETS. Knowing this, we cannot afford to be ignorant of his devices, seductions, and intentions to bring death and destruction to our lives **by any means necessary**. Remember, satan wants to attack your mind—your mind is the stumbling block. So, why is it that so many of God's called, appointed, and anointed ministers, musicians, psalmists, and dancers remain IN CAPTIVITY and BONDAGE to the flesh and all manner of SIN? Surely my co-laborers realize the impact to their souls, the Kingdom and the very Name of Jesus Christ. It must grieve and disgust the heart of the Father to see, feel, and know that even after He sent His Son to die for the very thing we struggle with, we still cannot call ourselves OVERCOMERS. It must STOP now—enough is enough!

Romans 8:28 tells us that "all THINGS work together for the good of those who love God, and are called according to His purpose. With that in mind, I recall the fact that I gave my life to Christ at the age of 24. While I made that decision consciously, I was nowhere near living a life of wholeness in mind, body, and spirit— that was pleasing to God. The mind is a serious thing. As the Rev. Grace Imathieu of Kenya stated in one of her sermons, "Sin is *sticky*. We must be careful not to become that which we hate". Although I had done the 'act' of giving my life to Christ, my mind was still stuck on sin. Much of this stickiness came from the fact that I, as a new Believer, continued to see and participate in the same behavior **in** the Church as I did outside. This observation is made so often and is agreed upon so widely amongst so called Christians and Believers—yet there are just a small number of individuals who will speak out and raise a standard of holiness that will not be lowered.

This is key to the life of ministry in which the sacred artist is released into. How are we are still permitted to knowingly serve and minister in our churches, national conferences, and international platforms while **actively engaged** in adultery, fornication, homosexuality, drugs, alcohol, common-law marriages, spousal abuse, child abuse, nightclub and dancehall life, foul language, smoking, binge eating, excessive dieting, financial fraud and thievery? Seemingly, we have become like society—desensitized in the House of God! Many ministers are operating under the 'don't ask, don't tell' mode of operandi! Our anointing is slipping because we have begun to mirror that which we hate. Just as with many of our beloved pastors and bishops in the pulpit, we are losing our accountability to anyone, and with that, our credibility to everyone.

Another area in which we must lay hold of discipline is in our views of self. Romans 12:3 says, "...and do not think of yourself more highly than you ought, but rather think of yourself with sober judgement in accordance with the measure of faith God has given to you." In our efforts to bring the sacred arts to the forefront of 21st Century Christian ministry, I sometimes wonder if we have 'created monsters'. There is a spirit of deception, pride, and competitiveness that lurks deep within the Arts ministry. This occurs mainly because many Christian artists who were professionally trained in the secular world have yet to totally surrender their Temples to the Holy Spirit. This total yielding far surpasses the performance ministry aspect. It encompasses the way we think, react, respond, and do business in the Body of Christ. Therefore, these deceptive and prideful spirits have propelled many individuals to self-elevation, false ordinations, manipulation, and jezebelian-like prostitution of one's gifts and anointing, in exchange for premiere bookings, title and name recognition, front row seating, and overall general preferential treatment. None of these exploits have one thing to do with the Kingdom.

> ## *Revelation:*
> **In confronting sin, we must be careful not to become the very things we say that we hate.**

Motives and Ministry

My brothers and sisters who engage in this type of 'networking' seem to have forgotten from whence they came. Discipline begins with recognition of what God saved us <u>out of</u>, and acceptance of the purpose for which God saved us <u>into</u>. This purpose cannot be a fleshy, self-marketing campaign, for reality tells us that in the end, all promotion comes from God. Rather, this discipline forces us to grow in grace, knowledge, and compassion for those who truly need ministry. This need surpasses the walls of the church (no matter how large the membership), national and international conferences, and star-studded Gospel concerts, whose target audiences are predominantly those who are already Believers.

Some of our beloved ministers and artists have been so busy creating names for themselves that they have seemingly neglected the small communities, ghettos, inner-cities, villages, and orphanages in which they emerged from, and, these very same persons are still in need of a Savior. We must be careful that as the Lord blesses, we do not fall into the deception that we have 'paid our dues'. Otherwise, it will be this attitude that will keep the seasoned dance ministers and artists from accepting ministry engagements in the above mentioned venues for fear that it would appear to be a backwards step for them on their campaign to 'stardom'. Worse, should a few misguided individuals accept an engagement to minister in one of these venues and actually expect to receive honorarium equivalent to that of a 10,000 member church!

Yes, the servant is worthy of his or her hire, but a true servant goes forth with the primary objective being to serve, not to get paid. There must be an ongoing, inner discipline throughout life in ministry that one ministers out of a grateful heart with no expectation of compensation. Only the Holy Spirit can guide you in exactly when to apply this principle. I believe with all my heart that God will honor and bless you abundantly for your obedience in this area. He alone knows when, how, and to what extent to bless our ministries and us financially. When this happens you will find yourself so abundantly blessed and prosperous—so much that you will give back to bless other organizations and ministries. In fact it will be as if you pay them for your opportunity to minister—not the other way around! THIS is true stardom with Kingdom purpose! We must also be aware that while financial blessing is wonderful, it is also a marvelous gift to be blessed with peace of mind. When Abraham offered his only son as a sacrifice to God in a spirit of discipline and absolute obedience he earned a high place in biblical history for generations to come:

> **"I swear by myself, declares the Lord, that because you have done this and have not withheld your son, your only son. I will surely make your descendants as numerous as the stars in the sky and as the sand on the seashore. Your descendants will take possession of the cities of their enemies, and through your offspring, all nations on earth will be blessed, because you have obeyed me." (Genesis 22:16-18)**

Discipline and obedience are a product of a yielded Temple (mind, body, and spirit) under the complete subjection to the Lordship of Jesus Christ and His teachings. The subjection is manifested through an alignment of our hearts with the heart of the Father. It is when our hearts are aligned with His that our bodies fulfil the will of God in action.

Spirit-Rituals, Disciplines, and Requirements of the Sacred Artist

There are sins that we have committed in our bodies years ago, that although completely delivered and set free, we continue to experience its backlash and repercussions. It's a deep **spiritual** thing. There are many types of 'spirit-rituals'—some healthy and some unhealthy. The sacred dancer must strive to maintain only the spiritual things that will produce a life of consecration and holiness to the Lord.

Before one can function effectively within their calling, there must be order. With that order, there must be accountability. When either of these two things are lacking, your ministry will suffer. Oftentimes, if someone would have just held us accountable—speaking the truth in love, satan's stronghold in our lives could have been broken and destroyed. It is a fact: without rules, there is wildness.

We become a virtual 'city without walls'; our boundaries open wider and wider; in essence, we become increasingly laxidazicle with our standards of excellence, holiness, and submission to God. This results in persons who 'minister' under the influence of drugs and alcohol, under spirits of condemnation, strife, rebellion, lust, depression, and fatigue—none of which allow the FULL MEASURE of a pure anointing by the Holy Spirit. Leaders, directors, and ministry heads: In evaluating your sacred dance or sacred arts ministry, consider the following self-examination for you and your members:

A. A BORN AGAIN EXPERIENCE WITH JESUS CHRIST:

As fundamental as this may sound, the reality is that not everyone who shows an interest in the dance ministry are born-again Believers. Just as everyone who comes to church regularly are not necessarily 'saved'. Because of the nature of the call to dance, the ministry attracts ALL KINDS—from ex-cheerleaders, to prostitutes, to strippers, to Broadway dancers. For some, the attraction is the fulfillment of a lost dream—that is, the individual always dreamed of being a ballerina, used to dance as a child but stopped, or cases where their previous church attended 'didn't believe in dancing'.

We must ask questions, not as critics, but as a matter of protecting God's property—His ministry that he has entrusted to us. "Are you saved?" "Since when?" "Tell me a little about how you came to know Jesus Christ". I think it's wonderful when a new Believer is called to the dance ministry. However, I do not recommend allowing that individual to minister immediately. Regardless of their technical gifting and anointing, there must be a period of time in which the person is *observed, taught and trained.* I suggest 3-6 months. (A sample interview/questionnaire for your arts/dance ministry can be found in the appendices of this book.)

No Other gods Allowed!

In some instances, the sacred dance ministry even attracts those who worship gods other than Jesus Christ. This happens more frequently than you think, and it is another strategy of satan to infiltrate and pervert God's ministry. A few years ago during a teaching seminar, I met a young woman who was quite taken with the whole idea and teaching on sacred dance. The Holy Spirit moved in wonderful ways through deliverance, outbreaks of joy, warfare, and repentance. While the name of Jesus Christ was being exalted throughout the seminar, this one young woman very quietly smiled, took notes, and from all outward appearances, she simply seemed 'shy'.

She told me how she'd trained as a professional dancer in college and how much she missed dancing. During our closing time of ministry and prayer, the woman came to me and with a very glazed over look on her face. She was visibly moved and wept as she began to talk about the "beauty of creation" and the "love of creation". She told me how wonderful I was and how my beauty was a reflection of creation. I responded "Thank you—Praise Jesus". I was not led to pray for her at that time.

One week later, I received a letter and a parcel package from this same woman in the mail. The package contained a beautifully designed, hand-made cross of white, gold, and pink stones with a figure engraved on it. The letter explained that she was a jewelry designer, and had especially made this cross for me based on the colors of my dance garments as displayed during the seminar.

The letter also was an invitation for two things:

    1) to minister in dance at her church

    2) to wear the cross whenever I ministered in dance

I continued reading all the niceties regarding her appreciation for my ministry, only to find at the end of the letter that she was a member of one of the largest Ba'Hai Churches in the city! **Now**, I prayed. The underlying intent of the enemy towards me as a vessel for the Lord Jesus Christ was a calculated attempt to engage me in idolatry. I was actually told by a few ministers whom I respected that they believed it would be a 'great witness' if I had accepted this invitation. Not so! This is where your discernment and reliability on the Holy Spirit must be active. In deciding to minister *anywhere*, the sacred dancer must know within his/her spirit if they should accept or decline. We've become so naive and caught up in our flesh that sometimes, the mere invitation to minister appeals to us and we find ourselves compromising our standards, our anointing, and our spiritual well-being. We can never be sure of one's motives, especially those who are not yet Believers. Who knows what kind of 'prayer', 'chant', or 'incantation' may have gone forth in the making of that piece of jewelry? What spirits would I have attracted as I wore it and danced? All that glitters is definitely not gold.

> # Revelation:
> Discipline and obedience are a product of a yielded Temple (mind, body, spirit) under complete subjection to the Lordship of Jesus Christ and His teachings ALONE.

B. SIGNS OF SPIRITUAL GROWTH MANIFESTED IN A TEACHABLE SPIRIT:

Matthew 7:17 says that a healthy tree produces MUCH fruit. And it's not just much fruit, it's good fruit that is our goal. When we don't produce much good fruit, the only thing left is either bad fruit, or no fruit at all. Rotten fruit is NOT an option. Faith comes by hearing and obeying the Word of God. The way that the dancer's faith and anointing increases is strictly by application of the Word of God in his or her life and the maintenance of a teachable spirit. Three basic principles in spiritual growth are as follows: reading the Word, prayer, and regular church attendance. For the Sacred Dancer, these must be fundamental. As we "grow up" from the nursing stage to adult stage in our relationship with Christ, we must constantly evaluate our progress HONESTLY. For some it will mean asking the Lord, "Father, am I pleasing you?" and then hearing His response. It will mean taking a hard look at the personal struggles, habits, and strongholds we had when we were first saved. Then, one must determine if now, two years, five years, or even 10 years later, there has been any deliverance. When the sacred dance minister offers his or her life up to God and welcomes Him to probe their innermost thoughts, motives, and actions, there is less chance that these same vessels will end up dancing before the throne of God, yet still BOUND. What must now be added is the *ability to receive from others*—mentors, teachers, pastors, elders; the ability to allow someone to pour positive Godly counsel into our lives. You can't give out what you don't have. This by no means implies that we copy, mimic, or impersonate those who have gone before us. Rather, it means that we are 'sifters'. Each individual must come to realize the following:

REVELATION DID NOT START WITH ME.
REVELATION DOES NOT END WITH ME.
ANOINTING DID NOT START WITH ME.
ANOINTING DOES NOT END WITH ME.
THERE IS ALWAYS SOMETHING MORE
    TO LEARN.
I MUST HAVE THE SPIRIT OF SUCCESSION.

A wise woman once told me, "One who has the spirit of a Dancer is a cut above the rest". It is not because we deem ourselves superior by any means. However, it is because we REALIZE that we have treasures in our earthen vessels! Even though others may not see it, it is a sense of security that the artists maintain. This surety will enable you not to feel insecure or intimidated by others whom God places in your path to make a significant contribution to your spiritual growth, and to your overall Kingdom purpose. When you are confident in this knowledge, it will compel you to live freely in the present, while having a worldview for the FUTURE concerning your ministry. Too many dance ministers do not have a *spirit of succession.* Succession means that one proactively and intentionally plans to leave a successful legacy and IMPRINT in Kingdom history by training, preparing, and imparting to others the ability to do what that individual is currently doing and to do *greater* works. Your ministry should not die when your mortal body leaves this Earth! Your ministry must have eternal implications in the Kingdom!

C. HUMILITY:

Humility is the true yielding and surrender of the dancer's soul to God. The area of humility must be conquered early in the dance minister's lifestyle and career. Understanding that many of the persons that God calls to this ministry were once professional artists in the secular world, if the flesh is not truly placed under the submission of the Holy Spirit, it can be very easy for these same sacred dance ministers to seek the applause of men, rather than the approval of God. It can also be very easy for the dancer to be drawn into the 'performance' of it all, while downplaying the aspect of ministry. This breeds a dangerous spirit of competition, rivalry, envy, and opportunism. All of these things are very carnal or 'fleshy' in nature.

As ministers of dance, we are blessed with the opportunity to minister alongside of some of the world's most anointed men and women of God. Ministry engagements with top recording artists, internationally known pastors and speakers, and worldwide invitations are a reality. However, in all of this, we must remember: satan hates virtue, meekness, humility. He despises it because when these characteristics are present in our lives, it becomes the place where God is glorified and where he stands up on the inside of us. Literally, we decrease, and He increases. To win the battle of humility, we must effectively strategize in spiritual warfare. We must know how to separate and discern those times when our OWN fleshly attitudes and actions are active, versus those which are strategically assigned to us from the devil. We can never blame all of our carnal actions on satan!

One guiding principle that is helpful when it comes to receiving the blessings of the Lord through promotion and recognition can be summed up in this: Never too impressed. Always be <u>very</u> thankful.

True humility will create a spiritual force field around your soul and protect you from the temptation and seduction of coveting another person's gifts. Humility will also keep you from prostituting your own gifts, talents, and your God-given anointing.

Once I was ministering during a large worship confer-ence. There was an internationally known Gospel recording artist in the audience on one particular night. A woman of God whom I had highly respected for many years was up to minister on this same night. She danced beautifully, invok-ing the presence of the Holy Spirit. Immediately following her time of ministry, the congregation remained in worship, still lifting up praises to God. It was at this time that the Lord allowed me to see an incident that opened my eyes to the reality of Christian carnality. During the worship, the young lady inconspicuously walked over to the Gospel artist, slipped him her business card, and gestured that he should call her!

Not only was it unsolicited, but it was inappropriate, and out of order! What was the Lord showing me? He was preparing me for the next lesson in spiritual disciplines of the sacred dancer—***honesty and integrity***.

D. HONESTY and INTEGRITY

This speaks to your true character. This is the 'real you', that is the person you are when you are not in front of a crowd, on the platform, or in church. This is you alone with *you*. It's that part of you that is admirable, fair, decent and good in heart. It's your ACTIONS, motives, and intentions. God knows your true heart—do you? The sacred artist must dare to see beyond the looking glass into the deep spiritual issues of life. This area will determine the future destination and success of your ministry. Ask yourself: Is my word reli-able? Can I be trusted? Am I one who tells lies? Is my flesh taking up more space than the Holy Spirit? Do I want a suc-cessful ministry by any means necessary? In other words, do you care whose toes you step on in your endeavors 'for

God', or will you strive to serve and minister to the Father in truth and righteousness?

Consider 2Corinthians 8:21, which says: "For we are taking great pains to do what is right, not only in the eyes of the Lord, but in the eyes of men." In ministry, no man or woman is an island. We must consider the hearts and sometimes, the emotions of those whom we relate to. I am not referring to a popularity contest, as I have discovered quickly in my own life that everyone will <u>not</u> like you. The sooner one embraces this reality, the better off they will be. However, we must also embrace Paul's admonishments in Romans 12:16-18 which says: "Live in harmony with one another. Do not be proud, but be willing to associate with people of low position. Do not be conceited. Do not repay anyone evil for evil; be careful to do what is right in the eyes of everybody, and if it is possible, as far as it depends on you, live at peace with everyone."

In leadership and in ministry, everyone will not agree with decisions you may make. One must be intentionally honest and of good moral character <u>as far as it depends on you</u>. Even the slightest infraction of character has the ability to make others stumble. If you are a leader in ministry, yet find it difficult to honor the Lord and his people with these basic values and expectations, please seek the Lord regarding immediate removal from your post or office. Maybe there are those who are living a lie right now—no one can minister in spirit and in truth if they are in bondage to a lie. Take time out now and ask the Lord's forgiveness in times when you have fell short in the areas of honesty and integrity. Allow the Holy Spirit to set you free in this area today:

LORD, I ACKNOWLEDGE THAT _____
_____.

Father, please forgive me.

FROM THIS DAY FORTH, I WILL _____

_____.

Lord, I give you ACCESS in this area of my life to change me in whatever ways necessary. Have your way, Father. AMEN.

E. 'BODY-TEMPLE' HEALTH

In the book of 3John verse 2, the Word of God says, "...Beloved, I pray above all things that you would prosper and be in good health even as your soul prospers." The Lord is vitally concerned about our bodies. It is His will that we maintain divine health in our bodies. However, this divine health cannot have its full measure of abundance in our lives without first having the wisdom, knowledge, and under-standing that we need to change the way we THINK. Romans 12:1-2 implores us "to present our bodies as a liv-ing sacrifice, holy and acceptable to God which is our rea-sonable service. And be not conformed to this world, but be transformed by the renewing of your mind..." Once we have a renewed mind concerning the prosperity of our physical and spiritual bodies, we will be able to win the war against poor health habits and harm to our bodies. Due to the nature of the arts ministry, the sacred artist is always positioned before the people of God. This is particularly true of the dance minister. This is a tremendous responsibility to uphold. Without delving deep into the secular world's stereotypical profile of a dancer, that is, petite, slim, small-breasted females or well-toned muscular males—I will men-tion that I believe that dancers can be effective in all shapes, sizes, and colors. However, I also believe that we must uphold a standard of good health, fitness, and welfare.

In Genesis 1:26, God said:

"Let us make man in our image, in our likeness,

and let them rule over the fish of the sea and the birds of the air, over the livestock, over all the earth, and over all the creatures that move along the ground. So, God created man in his own image, in the image of God he created him; male and female he created them. And God blessed them and said to them, "Be fruitful and increase in number; fill the earth, and subdue it..."

When God says, "let **them**" He is speaking of the all-inclusive male and female 'spirit-being', which He created. This spirit-being, called 'Adam' did not truly take form and manifest until God gave him a BODY. This body, or 'outer garment' is our Earth Suit. It is because of this outer garment called a body that we have been given the authority to subdue, rule, and have rightful dominion over the earth. That is why WE MUST KEEP OUR BODIES, SOULS, and SPIRITS HEALTHY AND HOLY UNTO GOD! When the body and soul are not experiencing full prosperity in the way they were created to, one becomes unproductive. The individual ceases to contribute to the life and well being of God's purpose here on earth, thus losing the RIGHT to have dominion in the earth. Where there is no dominion, death is nearby.

Satan is absolutely aware of the importance of the body. This is why he sends demons to seek out and occupy a *human earth suit or body*. Without one, they have no right to rule anywhere in the earth! And we know that when God manifested Himself through His Son Jesus Christ, He came into the world by way of an earth garment in the form of man. Our bodies are God's most important investment in the earth!

For the sacred dance minister, this revelation must be rooted in the core of our spirits. We must stop killing ourselves by active participation and over-indulgence of ungodly practices, whether it be over-eating, fasting with wrong motives, drug and alcohol abuse, chemical dependencies, sexual sin, lack of exercise, or neglect of spending time in the presence of the Lord. All of these affect your Body-Temple Health and well being— when not controlled will inevitably lead to all manners of disease and death.

In his book, *We Don't Die, We Kill Ourselves*, Christian medical doctor Cris Enriquez, M.D. outlines the Top 10 Causes of Death in the United States. He states that medical science confirms that all diseases are preventable, and that people die prematurely for two main reasons: disobedience and ignorance.

That is, of course, unless the purpose you were created for has been fulfilled. It is my prayer that these two things never be said of the sacred dance minister. Our source and pre-scription for the maintenance of a healthy, prosperous, and joy-filled life is found on the heels of the scripture sited in Exodus 15:20. This scripture is the first mention of dance in the Bible, and it comes after a glorious victory of the LORD as he parted the Red Sea:

"...And Miriam the prophetess, Aaron's sister, took up a tambourine in her hand, and all the women followed her with tambourines and dancing..."

A few lines down in verse 26, it reads:

"...And God said, If you listen carefully to the voice of the LORD your God and do what is right in his eyes, and if you pay attention to his commands and keep all his decrees, I will not bring on you any of the diseases I brought upon the Egyptians, for I am the LORD who heals you."

For Moses, Aaron, Miriam, and all the Isrealites, God

made a promise to grant healing and deliverance in exchange for obedience and praise. As Believers, we must claim this same promise for ourselves today from Jehovah Rapha—the Lord our Healer.

Revelation:
Your physical, emotional, and psychological healing and deliverance will rely upon the decisions you make in your obedience and attitude of praise.

F. ABILITY TO SUBMIT TO LEADERSHIP

Submission to leadership is a reality that all will face in their walk as Believers. When we submit, we are yielding ourselves to the spiritual counsel and guidelines set before us. This rule must not only be recognized in your place of employment, but also in your marriage, your family-life, your church, and your dance/arts ministry. This may sound repetitious and very basic, but the fact is that all of our work is done as unto the Lord. This is what aids us in dealing with ungodly employers and business practices.

As sacred arts ministers, you will be challenged in this area. Your ability or lack thereof, to submit to the leadership of the ministry can always be traced to a stronghold in the area of submission or control in your life. For those who walk victoriously in this area, the issue is resolved, and there is peace. The submission issue is only an opened wound for those who have not yet been made **whole.**

Once after ministering in dance at a convention, a young woman approached me and said that she seriously needed to talk with me. At the close of the worship experience, she came to me saying, "You really ministered to me. I have always believed that I had a call on my life to dance, and I really want to start by getting some good teaching." I shared with her concerning the Sacred Arts curriculum in which I was currently directing at Caribbean Christ for the Nations in Jamaica and she was very enthusiastic. After explaining that it was a 2-year programme, my eyes caught her hand and I noticed a wedding ring. "Are you married?" I asked. She replied positively. "Is your husband in ministry as well?" I inquired. She said, "No, he's not really a Christian." To that, I responded understandingly, "Oh. I see...that may be a bit tough to work out, though not impossible. The two of you would really have to talk about you going away to attend Bible School..." Her response went from calm to defensive in a hurry. "Talk about it? Why would it be difficult? Today, we women have more say in what we do...I will just tell him I want to do it, and that's it!"

Meanwhile, the Holy Spirit began to shout at me: "WRONG ATTITUDE", "OUT OF ORDER", and "REBELLIOUS" among other things. This woman definitely resented any hint at submission—godly or otherwise. If she had this attitude in her marriage, one could only imagine what attitude she may have had with her pastor. As a potential Bible School student and sacred artist, I'm sure this attitude would carry over into the classroom. No—she was definitely not ready.

As leaders in dance ministry, you will discover that many of your members are dancing as if they have the victory, but truly do not. Most resistance to submit to authority and leadership have three common sources with deadly implications:
1) Pride
2) Deception
3) Bitterness

If we are honest with ourselves and with God, we will admit that the building up of our defenses were laid in a foundation whose process was:
1) A hurt or an offense occurs—whether inside or outside of the Church.

2) Resentment sets in—we secretly crave revenge
3) A root of bitterness is developed in our spirits
4) Hatred and contempt is birthed in our hearts

At this stage in your ministry you will clearly observe the enemy launching strife and outright rebellion in your midst. The Bible reminds us, "For rebellion is as the sin of divination, and arrogance like the evil of idolatry..." (1 Samuel 15:23). The Spirit of Rebellion refuses the authority of leadership, thus the authority of God. And we know that rebellion must begin in the body (flesh) so that it has the ability to RULE over the person. As a minister of dance, you must be willing to submit to a line of authority similar to this: The Lordship of Jesus Christ, your godly spouse, your Pastor, your ministry leaders.

Although rebellion starts off in the heart of an individual, it spreads quickly. Rebellion is **infectious** and must not be tolerated in the Arts Ministry.

G. GLOBAL VISION for the WORLD

Proverbs 29:18 is true. Without a vision, the people will perish. We must have divine revelation in order to fulfill God's purpose in the earth. A vision must be acquired from the Holy Spirit through diligent and earnest communication. It is the ability to see, behold, take account, reflect, and MOVE towards that, which is of God. Therefore, the vision is prophetic—it has not yet manifested, but it is being summonsed by the Holy Spirit through US. One cannot last long in dance or any other ministry without Kingdom-centered vision. Some of our ministries die prematurely because the vision was too small and there was no acknowledgement that the World had a vital part to play in God's assignment. This is what has happened to many of the churches in the United States. Many of my brothers and sisters in ministry actually believe that America IS the WORLD. Therefore, they have superficial interest or none at all in what's going on outside of their borders. But the World is all of humankind. It is a geographical recognition of the spiritual and moral climate accompanied with the present condition of humanity. When one loses site of this, the ministry to God's people loses its relevance. Therefore, ones message in sacred artistry will have no prophetic value whatsoever. If you want to be effective, relevant, and experience longevity in this type of ministry, you must develop a global vision and perspective concerning your relationship to God and His World. How does this occur? The Bible tells us that we must study to show ourselves approved. This study speaks to preparation. God will not use you internationally until He confirms that you heart has been immersed in purity. The heart of a global-minded individual is softened towards the people of a particular nation, while at the same time remains realistic to its troubles, challenges, and dysfunction. One must do their 'homework' as it applies to the world. Become acquainted with world maps, religions, cults, ethnic groups, languages, governmental systems, and the needs of the poor. It is never too late, nor too soon to cultivate global aware-ness. Over the past two years, the Lord birthed a Christian Arts and Missions program for children called, "Seed to the Nations". Once per week, the children received the imparta-tion and teaching of sacred dance forms, drama, storytelling, Christian puppetry, missions and intercession. Each week a new nation was highlighted in an atmosphere of learning and prayer. By the end of the 16-week semester, the children were able to recite the names of various nations, their reli-gious make-up, the struggles they faced environmentally and economically, and particularly, any persecution suffered for being a Christian. At the end of each session, the class spent time interceding for the children of that country. The children then created a group dance dedicated to those chil-dren who cannot dance themselves. It was life changing for them, as well as for me as their instructor! The youngest member of the class was 3 years old! One can never be too young to speak a prophetic prayer of liberation and freedom for the world.

Revelation:
Your Vision becomes your Mission once your vision is CAPTURED. Therefore, only do those things that are related to your purpose. This way, you will know who and what NOT to TOUCH. You must be conscious of what and where your Kingdom Destination resides. This will help you not to make wrong turns.

H. LOVE AND COMPASSION FOR GOD'S PEOPLE

Love is not only a command from God, but true love is also a discipline. It must be purposefully practiced and experienced in your life in order for it to be effective in your ministry. In John 11:33, the Bible tells us how Jesus was "moved with compassion", to the point of weeping concerning the death of Lazarus. Compassion is something that must move us to action. For the sacred dance minister, if we lack a true and genuine love and compassion for the people of the world, our ministry efforts will be in vain. These two things will determine our destinies because it speaks to our hidden motives and attitudes. The dance minister cannot live a double life. When you do not have sincere love and compassion for your ministry team members and the Church, it will surely reveal itself in your ministry performance. Why? Because the Holy Spirit must reign supreme in our hearts and without love, compassion, and conviction the anointing will be depleted. There are many ministers who are functioning in leadership roles who are just NOT nice people.

They are, in fact, mean, hard to get along with, unapproachable, short-tempered, and arrogant. Yet, still blinded by the so-called 'love' that they have for Jesus, continue to believe that they can minister effectively in sacred dance. "Afterall," they say, "I'm ministering unto the LORD." But the Bible says in 1John 4:20-21, "...if anyone says, "I love God", yet hates his brother, he is a liar and the truth is not in him. For anyone who does not love his brother, whom he has seen, cannot possibly love God, whom he has not seen." If you believe that you are called to this ministry, yet you have issues with loving your fellowman or woman, think again— maybe you've missed God.

I. <u>COMMITMENT</u>

Commitment is directly related to **giving.** When we make the decision to get saved and become members of a local church Body, we are no longer 'visitors'. Our level of commitment goes to an entirely different dimension. For most churches, this may mean attending new members class, joining an accountability prayer group, regular attendance at Bible study, tithing, and working in the ministry area of your calling.

This parallel of commitment and giving can also be reflected in many other life circumstances: acceptance of a new position at work, getting married, and deciding to have children. In all, the commitment we make speaks volumes of what we are prepared and willing to share of our lives with others.

Whether it is of our time, talents, or finances, the sacred arts minister must develop and maintain a high level of commitment. This commitment begins by putting your call to ministry in its proper context and prioritization. Oftentimes we become so committed to a thing, a person, or an organization that we lose ourselves in the process. In Psalm 37:5, we are charged to "commit all our ways to the Lord, and He will make our paths straight." In giving of ourselves to the ministry, the realization is that we give OURSELVES fully to God and the structure he has placed in authority over us. This structure may include things like prayer time, extended rehearsals, counseling, teaching, missions and ministry outreaches, and challenging schedules of ministry engagements. However, it may also include the 'menial' tasks like garment maintenance (sewing, washing, ironing, etc.), sweeping and cleaning the rehearsal space, and **timely** arrival to rehearsals. All of this is part of your commitment in giving yourself to the sacred arts ministry. While God is building and establishing order, He will begin to delegate certain people for certain areas, however, NONE OF US must be unwilling to do even the simplest task if called upon. This commitment is a testing ground for you as an up-and-coming Levite in the Glorious Priesthood of sacred artistry.

J. HOLY SPIRIT FILLED

This is an area of much discussion and controversy between the various denominations and sacred artistry ministries. In short, my summary of this requirement encompass two items:
1. Having a personal, intimate relationship with the Holy Spirit
2. Having received the baptism of the Holy Spirit with the evidence of speaking in tongues

Personal, Intimate Relationship with the Holy Spirit

As Believers, or those who have been born again, the assurance of our salvation is often articulated according to Romans 10:9 that we confessed the Lordship of Jesus Christ with our mouths and believed in our hearts that God raised Him from the dead. The next manifestation of our salvation is in the fact that we have a "personal relationship with Jesus Christ". In other words, we know Him and He knows us—

intimately. We are in regular communion and fellowship with Him. The requirement of a personal relationship with the Holy Spirit lies in the fact that Jesus told us in the book of St. John Chapters 14 to 16 that in His going, He will send us another Counselor, that is the Spirit of Truth , who does the following:

- The Holy Spirit teaches and reminds us of everything Jesus spoke (John 14:26)
- The Holy Spirit testifies about Jesus (John 15:26)
- The Holy Spirit convicts the world of sin, righteousness, and judgment (John 16:8)
- The Holy Spirit guides us into all truth. (John 16:13)
- The Holy Spirit tells of things yet to come. (John 16:13)
- The Holy Spirit brings glory to Jesus Christ. (John 16:14)

Without a personal relationship with the Holy Spirit, none of these things can be fully experienced in your life and ministry. In fact, your dancing should strive to achieve the above attributes. It is solely with the help and anointing of the Holy Spirit that your dances will have purpose and impact on earth and in eternity.

As you are inspired to create and choreograph new artistic works, be sure to do a quick assessment to ensure that the Holy Spirit is operating within your particular art form according to the Word of God.

Having Received the Baptism of the Holy Spirit with the Evidence of Speaking in Tongues

This is not included as a discipline for the purpose of sounding 'spiritual' or trying to impress anyone or any particular denomination. It is included as a matter of the writer's personal belief, revelation, and the manifestation of the miraculous in my life. Before I received the baptism of the Holy Spirit, I already believed the Word in Ephesians 3:20 which says that, "God is able to do exceeding, abundantly, above all things that we could ever ask or think according to the *power* that is at work within us." However, it took time for me to get the revelation that it was not *my own* power and strength that God is referring to. The true sacred artist and dance minister is a called intercessor. In order to get in the position of interceding for oneself and for others, you must DESIRE TOTAL surrender your mind, intellect, reasoning, opinions, and soul to the wisdom and authority of the Holy Spirit. This willingness is what gives the sacred arts minister—particularly the dance minister—his or her VOCAL prayer language, as well as their BODY-prayer language. Consider Romans 8:26 and note the writer's correlation between dance and intercession as symbolized with the asterisk (*):

"In the same way, the Spirit helps us in our weakness. We do not know what we ought to pray* (dance) for, but the Spirit himself intercedes* (dances) for us with groans* (movements) that words cannot express. And he who searches our hearts knows the mind of the Spirit, because the Spirit intercedes* (dances) for the saints in accordance with God's will." This groaning will manifest according to the level in which the Spirit is given room to break forth—whether in wailing, utterances, weeping, or tongues—the Spirit Knows.

This is Power! The Holy Spirit must come "up-ON" us (Acts 1:8) in order for us to experience the fullness of the power that God has bestowed and placed in our 'Body-Temples'.

K. EMBRACE WORSHIP AS A LIFESTYLE

Who are you really? When you're alone and nobody is there to observe, criticize, admire, or serve you—who are you? How do you *really worship* God? When you are not at church, in the choir, or in the pulpit—when the spotlight is not on you, who are you really? Our lifestyles represent our values, morals and beliefs. For the sacred dancer, these must line up with the Word of God. We must strive to be 'above reproach' with God and man. Ministers who live double lifestyles will surely cut the flow of the anointing and blessings in their lives.

This 'double life' is plaguing the Church Universal. HIV/AIDS has crept into so many of our congregations at proportionate numbers as a result of promiscuity, adultery, and homosexuality practiced right under our noses. Pastors and elders attempt to preach righteousness on Sunday mornings and then go home to physically and sexually abuse their wives and children. False prophets travel the world with charismatic drama productions disguised as revelation knowledge and ministry to God's people. Leaders are running all over the country to be seen at international conferences and minister to the masses while their marriages and families are being neglected and torn apart. Pastors can no longer teach and preach effectively on marriage, relationships, celibacy, or divorce because so many of them have already had multiple relationships during their pastorate. So-called Christian organizations publicly endorse unity in the Body and the nations, while privately they continue to perpetuate subtle discrimination, supremacy, and racism. I believe the heart of God is sickened by what His eyes behold. If we continue to present the façade of holiness and purity while our true lifestyles are an abomination to the Father, there will be no true remnant with clean hands to carry the legacy of the priesthood into the next generation.

<u>Prayer Declaration:</u>

Dear Father,
You have given me an awesome gift, and with that comes much responsibility.
Today I commit myself to an even deeper, more intimate relationship with You;
Your Word says that to whom much is given, much is required; so Lord, I thank you now for your compassion and loving correction;
Thank You for Your Holy Spirit who leads and guides me into all Truth for Your Name's sake;
Help me to consecrate my body to You daily as a living sacrifice;
Help me to keep it holy and acceptable unto You, Lord.
In Jesus' Name,
Amen.

Reader's Reflections:

(Fill in your own personal statements of affirmation.)

My Affirmations:

I will discipline myself concerning _____

_____

_____

My most difficult obstacle in achieving this is _____

_____

I will take the first step by _____

_____

_____

Sacred AFFIRMATION #7

I AM Born to Flow in Worship.
I WILL Not Live in the Outer Court!
I AM Ready to Move when the Spirit Commands.
I COME to the Throne of God with Reverent
BOLDNESS!

CHAPTER SEVEN

Integration of Sacred Dance and Artistry to the Total Worship Experience

"Your procession has come into view, O God, the procession of my God and King into the sanctuary. In front are the singers, after them, the musicians; and with them are the maidens playing the tambourines. Praise God in the great congregation; praise the Lord in the assembly of Israel." (Psalm 68:24-26)

We must now move to a place where what occurs during church is no longer known as the 'Worship Service', rather the ' Worship Experience'. For the worshipper, it is impossible to "do" church. It must be an all-encompassing, 'trinitarian' experience between you, the Father, the Son, and the Holy Spirit.

Too often, Believers take church so much for granted that in calling it a worship service, they begin to subconsciously view church attendance as a job, a responsibility, or something that is done out of a sense of obligation. When this type of attitude is present within the House of God, it becomes impossible for the Holy Spirit to have full reign in the minds, bodies, and spirits of the congregants. Many will resist new or different moves of the Spirit because in the past, they have known exactly what to expect throughout their precious church time. Anything outside of the ordinary tradition is viewed as unnecessary, emotionally intrusive, 'not the way we normally do it', and therefore, requires a special board meeting in which a formal vote may be taken. There are also those members who have served faithfully in the same church for years and long for a fresh wind of the Holy Spirit to clear out the mental baggage and bondage which has accumulated over time. Therefore, as the ministry of dance and sacred artistry goes forth, it is essential that the hearts of the people be prepared. This must be done through anointed teaching and demonstration on how to integrate God's creative revelation, His artistic expression, and His Word to bring about a true 21st Century Worship Experience.

As the power of sacred dance is further recognized across various cultures and denominations, it becomes imperative that this integration into the church setting is done in excellence to the glory of God. There are many different styles of worship programming, otherwise called the Order of Worship. Throughout the Church Universal, the Order of Worship may vary according to culture, denomination, or pastoral preference. The following is just one example of an Order of Worship, including definitions and basic characteristics of each item. Keep in mind that the ultimate variation in any Order of Worship is an alteration brought on only by the prompting of the Holy Spirit. Note how sacred dance and artistry may be strategically and effectively used throughout the programming to enhance, heighten, compliment, and bring the overall worship experience to another dimension.

Proposed Order of Worship

Prelude: a time of meditation, reflection, and preparation in silent prayer; the prelude occurs at the beginning of the worship experience and is usually accompanied by soft, instrumental music.

Incorporate Dance/Movement:

A small group (2-4) of dancers may fill the front or platform area by doing movements of reverence. These movements may include positions of prostration, prayer and welcoming of the presence of God individually or collectively. This may be accomplished with soft music of worship in the background.

Invocation: the opening, corporate prayer in which the Holy Spirit is summoned, welcomed, and invoked to rule in authority over the worship service and the worship participants.

Incorporate Dance/Movement:

a) **The Dance of Invocation must be one that specifically invites the presence of the Holy Spirit in the song selected and the movements executed. There are many songs that accomplish this and can be brought together with dance as a powerful initiator of the Spirit. It can serve as the same, if not more than, the purpose of the spoken invocation.**

b) **Another option may be a combination spoken prayer (by the minister or laity) while the dance minister interprets the prayer through movement. This is powerful!**

Procession: ceremonial movement which occurs at the beginning of the worship experience; the processional symbolizes the gathering of God's people in preparation for the corporate worship service; usually consists of a musical

selection or hymn at which time the choir, clergy, and all
other worship participants move to their positions.

Incorporate Dance/Movement:
**In 2Samuel 10:5, the Bible speaks of a procession of
prophets who came down from the high place rejoicing
and prophesying with tambourines, flutes, harps. Psalm
68:25 also speaks of the grand procession of singers,
musicians, and dancers into the sanctuary.**

**The procession is a symbol of triumph. The dance minis-
ters and worship participants who are in the procession
may do so with streamers, banners, batons, or nothing at
all. The procession may initially come forth in multiple,
single lines of uniform movement, and may move into
other formations such as circles, diagonals, boxes, or
arrows. The formations and spirit of the procession
should be celebratory, upbeat, and victorious in nature.**

**Specifically, leading the procession should be the musi-
cians, next the choir (or singers), then the sacred artists,
and finally the priests, ministers, and all other clergy.
The procession may initially begin with a pre-recorded
music selection and as the musicians and singers get into
position, they continue with live praise. This is a wonderful, vibrant way to enter His courts with thanksgiving
and praise! Also, it prepares and charges the atmosphere
for worship.**

Praise and Worship: the time set aside for the psalmist(s),
choir, musicians, and dancers lead the congregation into the
presence of the Lord; the time in which the atmosphere is
consecrated and the people are prepared to receive the Word
of God. This is accomplished through the external act of
vocal praise and the internal manifestation of intimate wor-

ship. Praise is both descriptive (speaking of God's attributes and characteristics) and declarative (proclaiming and confirming what God has done and will do). It is also during this time of praise when the Holy Spirit may lead the congregation into a time of intense intercession and warfare leading into the worship.

Our worship is demonstrating personal adoration and reverence for God which may be expressed through prostration, stretching of the arms, kneeling, bowing down, or whatever the Spirit compels one to do.

Incorporate Dance/Movement:
One powerful and effective way to engage the entire church in full praise and worship is through the use of congregational dance. Stylized movement and expressive praise will accomplish this. Stylized movement is simple, repetitive movement combinations, which are modified so that the young and the old may praise God corporately. Expressive praise may be the use of specific gestures, especially modified sign language, which is easy to follow. Using movement and dance during times of praise and worship releases the pastors, leaders, and the congregation to vibrant participation in joyful worship to God. It also assists in releasing a corporate anointing similar to that of praying 'on one accord'.

Scripture Reading (s): time in which the Word of God is read aloud, either singly or corporately; the reading of God's Word is usually done through one selected text from the Old Testament and one from the New Testament. The selected texts will usually correlate with the sermon to be delivered by the man or woman of God.

Incorporate Dance/Movement:
The interpretation of the reading of the scripture through

movement carries a special anointing when done with power, clarity, and authority. Only the dance minister who KNOWS the Word of God thoroughly and confidently should attempt to minister the scriptures in dance. The movement that comes forth must have a certain level of depth and understanding with it. The movements must compliment the reading, not distract from it. The dancer should have an extensive movement vocabulary and be able to change movement thoughts at short notice, while maintaining the anointing.

Selection or Special Item: an artistic solo, instrumental, choral, dance, or dramatic interpretation ministered to God's people in order to inspire, ignite, comfort, or encourage. The selection could either be in the nature of praise or worship, depending on the flow of the service thus far, and the leading of the Holy Spirit.

Incorporate Dance/Movement:
While this is already happening all over the world, I still feel it necessary to state. Special ministry items and selections should be alternated between the soloists, choirs, dramatists, and the DANCERS. If your church leadership is constantly calling upon the musicians and singers to do a 'selection' while appearing to ignore or to exclude the dancers, dramatists, and mimes, this is definitely an item for prayer. We must remind one another of God's Word which tells us that the Father seeks TRUE worshippers—not performers. Therefore, whatever ministry item is chosen, it is the sacred artist's responsibility to minister to God FIRST; then, allow Him to bless the people.

> ## *Revelation:*
> **The Holy Spirit is the True Worship Leader of the Church. Any variation or alteration in the Order of Worship must be prompted and approved by Him.**

<u>Tithes and Offering:</u> the opportunity given to the congregation to give monetarily of what God has blessed and provided them with. Depending on the size of the congregation, the offering times are either facilitated by the appointed ushers who serve each row, or by standing in front of the church and allowing the congregates to come forward uniformly and orderly.

Incorporate Dance/Movement:

a) **This should be viewed as a time of continuous worship, praise, and celebration. If the congregation is being served at their seats, this is a perfect time for a lively group ministry piece, which could engage the congregation in dance as well. As individuals have given, they may be invited to stand and join the dancers in congregational movement. This invitation to join in the praise allows the spirit of a 'cheerful giver' to flow even more freely. Afterwhich, the congregation may continue standing for the prayer/ blessing of the offering.**

b) **As the ushers direct, the pastor or worship leader may encourage the congregants to 'dance' forward with their offering—a true "sacrifice of praise" for our more conservative brothers and sisters, but a joy to behold!**

c) **Aside from a specific dance done concerning giving, this portion of the worship experience may also be**

demonstrated through the use of dramatization and short skits.

Sermonic Selection: a choir or a soloist has traditionally done this selection. The sermonic selection is meant to stir up the ministry gifts in the speaker who will minister, as well as to stir God's people. This selection should be done in accordance to the Word that will go forth OR the spirit in which the service is currently flowing. For example, if the Holy Spirit has been ministering in the area of warfare or healing, then the sermonic selection may continue in that direction.

Incorporate Dance/Movement:
When the sermonic selection is done through the use of sacred dance, it must prepare the ground for the Word of God. It must also prepare the hearts of the people to receive the Word. One way that the dancer may work in collaboration with the flow of the service is to inquire of the general tone of the speaker's message ahead of time.

If the dance minister knows the main topic, scripture reference, or general tone of the message, this can be quite helpful and very powerful in setting the atmosphere for the Word. There are special times when the Holy Spirit may move so powerfully in the sermonic dance that the speaker will be inspired to either continue in the flow of worship and praise (i.e. no spoken, preached Word goes forth). Alternately, the speaker may be led to change his or her message altogether based on what God is saying through the dance. This requires a truly humble and yielded heart on the part of the pastor or speaker.

Sermon: this is the pivotal point in the worship service in which the minister proclaims the Good News of Jesus Christ through the preaching and teaching of His Word.

Incorporate Dance/Movement:

A sermon can be preached, taught, or danced powerfully through the creative innovation of the Holy Spirit. A team of 4-7 dance ministers may develop and build a sermon through the combined usage of the spoken word and dance interpretation, based on a pre-selected scriptural text.

The combined usage of speech and movement should only be executed by dance ministers or dramatists who are confident and anointed in this area. It is especially effective when done by those sacred artists who are also called to the preaching ministry, as they may more readily be equipped to exegete a given text creatively.

While the practice of dancing a sermon may not be the norm, there may be special occasions or specific Sundays in which the Arts is showcased to the glory of God—this would be a great blessing because it would demonstrate the radicality and diversity of our God!

Invitation to Christian Discipleship or Altar Call: it is at this time that the opportunity is given for lost souls to give their lives to Jesus Christ. The man or woman of God usually extends the invitation. This will usually reiterate significant points in the sermon, while tying them in with the need for salvation. The invitation or 'altar call' can also serve as an opportunity for Believers to repent, receive forgiveness, and deliverance. It is at this sensitive point in the worship experience that the Holy Spirit moves to convict and convince individuals of their sins, need of repentance, and decision to give their lives to Christ.

Incorporate Dance/Movement:
The dance of invitation may be done after or during the initial, spoken invitation to salvation. It is like unto the musical selection usually done during the invitation. This can be very powerful and effective in sealing the message that has gone forth. Some may view this concept as distracting, since in our man-made traditional church programming, nothing occurs after the Word has gone forth. On the contrary, there is no real biblical basis for this practice. In some cases, this ministry in movement may be the deciding factor in winning a lost soul to Christ. Therefore, the dance of invitation must be evangelistic in nature. In its song, movements, and actions, it must carry the anointing and burden to save souls. Utilization of the invitational dance is especially effective during street ministry.

Benediction The closing prayer and blessing given by the minister over God's people. The benediction and blessing may be declarative or prophetic in nature. It seals and confirms all that occurred in the service and in the individual.

Incorporate Dance/Movement:
Just as in the opening prayer or invocation, there may be a combination of the spoken prayer (by the minister or laity) and the dance minister(s) who interpret the blessing over God's people through movement. One beautiful benediction to interpret through movement is the doxology found in Jude verse 24: "To Him who is able to keep you from falling and to present you before his glorious presence without fault and with great joy—to the only God our Savior be glory, and majesty, power and authority, through Jesus Christ our Lord, before all ages, now and forevermore! AMEN"

<u>Recessional:</u> the recessional occurs at the close of the worship experience. It is celebratory, ceremonial movement done to a song or musical selection in which the choir, clergy, and other worship participants formally retire from the service. The recessional symbolizes the dispersing of God's people into the world for mission and ministry.

<u>Incorporate Dance/Movement:</u>
What a great opportunity for the whole Church to REJOICE! This experience should move the congregation to a new dimension of victory and challenge for the week to come. It's not only a Commission to us individuals, but also a reminder to the devil that he is defeated! Therefore, the congregational dance that is executed may begin with the dance ministry and other worship participants, but may spill over to a time of 'free praise' to the congregation. The worshippers should actually <u>dance</u> their way out of the House of God!

Revelation:

When my concept of 'church' changes to include God's Creative Character, I will SEE manifestation of supernatural healing, deliverance, growth, prosperity, hunger for God, and uncommon MIRACLES.

There are so many wonderful, biblical ways that God has given us to worship Him in the Arts. He is restoring Sacred Arts to the Church, but it will take much prayer, intercession, and <u>teaching</u> in order for dance to be fully embraced and utilized for its original purpose—that is, praise, worship, celebration, and warfare. In the interim, dance ministers and sacred artists must also be willing to tear down the walls and boundaries of the church building by establishing open-air street meetings in needy neighborhoods, inner-cities, theatres, and communities where the Gospel needs to be heard via evangelistic ministry and missions outreach. The Arts serve as one of God's chosen weapons in the Kingdom. Pastors, clergy persons, and church leaders will be instrumental in the perception, recognition, and acceptance of sacred dance and the Arts during the traditional worship experience. They must come to the revelation that the Sacred Arts are not exclusively for the Easter Pageant, the special Christmas Service, or the Mother's Day prayer breakfast. Sacred dance and artistry carries an anointing that is far too large to be contained and manipulated at the whim of man. As sacred dance ministers, we have a responsibility to continuously educate and demonstrate to the World this unique gift that God has given His Church. We must carry our mantles in holiness for the sake of our children of the next generation.

Prayer Declaration:

Father, thank You that You are a Creative Wonder! I thank You now for a supernatural impartation of creativity and innovation in my worship and in the worship of churches all over the world; Help us to lean not unto our own man-made understanding, but to yield to Your Holy Spirit as we work all of the gifts together for the good of Your children and the good of Your Church. Thank You, Lord for the fresh and renewing inspiration of the Spirit of Praise! In Jesus' Name, AMEN.

Reader's Reflections:

(Fill in your own personal statements of affirmation.)

My Affirmations:

I feel inhibited during worship when _____

_____

_____

I will overcome this by attempting to _____

_____

_____

I will make my sacrifice of praise _____

_____

_____

Sacred AFFIRMATION #8:

I AM a Vessel of Calmness in a World of Chaos!
I WILL Guard My Heart and Mind from Confusion!
I BRING a New Level of Excellence to
the World of Sacred Artistry!
I AM an Eternal Blessing to
the Body of Christ!

CHAPTER 8

Administration, Decency and Order in the Ministry

"For though I am absent from you in body, I am present with you in spirit, and I delight to see how orderly you are and how firm your faith in Christ is." Colossians 2:5

In the administration of any dance ministry or Arts ministry team, there must be <u>order.</u> The presence of order and stability will deter and diffuse many of the tactics that the enemy will attempt to bring into our midst. How difficult is it for you to imagine that God is present and watching your response and reaction to chaotic situations? God is not the author of confusion. In other words, He does not create it. However, the Spirit of God is definitely observing our responses. The way in which we manage our lives will reflect the way in which we manage our ministries. In order to flow in the spirit of excellence, one must have the gift of administration operating through them either as a dominant or as a secondary gift.

Appointing a Leader

For a long time, I never understood why I did things in the manner in which I did them. I have always been very methodical in my approach to any task. I'm sure that many individuals can relate to this description: you know what you want, how you want it done, and will execute your plan 'to the tee' until its completion. Sometimes, persons who fit this description are negatively looked upon as 'control freaks', and even a bit over-bearing. Have you ever been accused of being this type of individual? I am not condoning any behavior that is overbearing and manipulative of others. However, I do affectionately endorse these qualities as "gifts" which must be utilized, *accompanied by* the fruits of the Spirit. Galatians 5:22 clearly defines how we must handle one another in the Spirit of love, joy, peace, patience, kindness, goodness, faithfulness, gentleness, and, my favorite, SELF-CONTROL. While some manifest their leadership roles through subtle control and manipulation of others, I'm convinced that the first sign of a potential leader is one who demonstrates self-control in every sense of the word. Consider 1Thessalonians 4:11-12:

> **"Make it your ambition to lead a quiet life, to mind your own business, and to work with your hands, just as we told you, so that your own daily life may win the respect of outsiders and so that you will not be dependent on anybody."**

Leading a 'quiet life', 'minding one's own business', and 'working with your own hands' should not be interpreted as being isolated and solely concerned about you and your family. Rather, each of these commands speaks to a Believer's responsibility to strategize for the Kingdom of God. Continuously practicing self-control breeds a mind with supernatural focus on that which is relevant. One will acquire the ability to go into their personal secret place with God in order to receive instruction and revelation concerning what the Father would have them to accomplish. Many of the greatest leaders in the world were not those who had the biggest mouths. They were not those who were involved in every political and social conflict that came about. Nor were they the ones who were even the most charismatic and eloquent in speech. There will be times to roar, but there will also be times to purr. A good leader has wisdom to know the difference.

Individuals who allow the Holy Spirit to utilize their gifts of administration are usually blessed with an anointing to be highly effective and productive. The ability to *produce results qualitatively and effectively* is key to one's success. This is another necessity in becoming an effective leader of any ministry or organization. When the Lord gave me this revelation, it was only then that I could stop beating myself up for being the way that God created me! While serving in Jamaica, I learned a song that says:

> *"I am God's work of art, created to live forever;*
> *I am God's work of art, created to live forever;*
> *It was the LORD who formed me in the womb;*
> *It was the LORD who set my spirit free;*
> *It will be the LORD who's coming back for me—*
>   *Just for ME!*
> *I AM God's work of art, created to live forever!"*

As we sang this song directly to one another during times of praise and worship, the liberating power of the Holy Spirit began to set many of us free to be ourselves! I realized that each of us is God's 'work of art' and that He knew exactly how He needed to design us in order for us to fulfill our destinies! Once we realize **who we *really* are**, it drives our ability to discipline ourselves within the path God has chosen for us. This discipline may even extend to the very name we are called by. For example, my last name, Butler means 'one who is given authority'. It also means, 'one who is a high-ranking administrator'. My first name, Stephanie, comes from 'Stephanos', which means 'one who is crowned for success or victory'! I'm sure that my parents did not realize what they were doing when they named me, but God knew! Before I was even thought about, He knew ME! Therefore, my very *name* points me to my destiny, but my success is contingent upon my obedience to manage and steward all that has been placed in my authority.

Revelation:
There will be times to roar, AND times to purr—A good leader has the wisdom to know the difference.

The leadership of an Arts Ministry is absolutely critical. Just as a pastor is the shepherd of his or her flock, under the authority of God, so is the leader of the arts ministry. He or she must be in good standing, both in the church and the community. The individual must be under the covering of a Pastor who is submitted to the Word of God. Therefore, the leadership of the church may desire to appoint and or give their official blessing to ministers of the Arts because it is a ministry of the church. Sacred Artists must be given over to training, discipline, and study of the Word in order to perfect their gift. This requires much prayer, rehearsal, fellowship, and time.

As leaders in the Arts ministry, one must be able to lead in excellence without losing sight of the fact that the ministry does not belong to us—it is God's property. Your leadership must be woven around a strong rod of capable, loyal administrators. For those individuals who are directors of arts ministries, but absolutely do NOT have the gift of administration, it is imperative that he or she appoints an administrator who is both qualified and anointed for the task.

Your Gift Will Make Room For You

Proverbs 18:16 says, "Your gift will make room for you and bring you into the presence of the great..." Sometimes, the Holy Spirit will appoint a leader from within, and it will be obvious to all those involved. Usually, this is the individual who possesses a special and unique gift to:

1) Minister under the Anointing
2) Execute plans administratively (i.e. excellent organizational skills, communication skills, dedication, and commitment)
3) Teach others with clarity, authority, and understanding
4) Produce results successfully
5) Communicate the Vision and direction in which God wants the ministry to go

It will not be by your own doing or 'maneuvering' that appointment to leadership will come. Only through the faithful, diligent working of the gifts and talents that God has given an individual will, he or she emerge as a leader among leaders. True leaders in Christian ministry will not compromise themselves in order to receive special treatment, accolades, or promotion. They lift up the Name of Jesus in every aspect of their lives, whether personal or professional, and then allow His name to draw all others to them.

Ministry Staffing: Artistic vs. Administrative

Administration

Just as any other church ministry or auxiliary that is active within the Church body, the Arts ministry must have this administrative aspect to it. There should be harmony, driven by clear role definition of each ministry member.

The following is a model of one way that your ministry may be structured in order to maximize its effectiveness. The model is dynamic, so it can be adjusted to fit the size and personality of your specific ministry team. First, distinguish between those positions that call for Artistic Staff vs. those which call for Administrative Staff. In the area of Artistic Staff, your team may look similar to the following:

Artistic Staff:

Director: This person leads, guides, and directs the overall spiritual formation, creative, and technical aspects of the Arts Ministry. He or she is responsible for the 'shepherding' of the group, and general welfare of its members as it relates to their growth and development while serving on the team. As the senior person in authority, it is the director's responsibility to provide clear, godly vision and structure for the team. All outside team ministry engagements should be accepted or declined through the Director. The Director must be under the covering of his/her local church body, thus receiving the blessing of his/her pastor to minister.

Assistant Director: This individual is responsible for leading the ministry team in every capacity as needed in the absence of the Director. He or she must assist the Director in bringing forth God's vision for the ministry. Aside from assuming the Director's role during their absence, the Assistant Director should serve as a key intercessor for the Director and the team. Therefore, this individual is extremely important, and must be chosen with much prayer and discernment applied via the Director and if necessary, the pastor. The Assistant Director should also be designated as the key coordinator for special conferences, seminars, and workshops either hosted by the Ministry Team, or planned for the team's further enrichment.

Worship Leader: The Worship Leader for the Arts Ministry team is responsible for opening every meeting, rehearsal, or gathering in a time of devotion. This may be done through song, prayer, intercession, sharing, or however the Holy Spirit leads. The Worship Leader should coordinate with the Director in the planning of designated times of Bible Study or special topics to be covered during meeting times as needed.

Chaplain: The Chaplain serves as the team's spiritual advisor and counselor. He or she coordinates Bible studies, times of prayer and intercession, and provides special counsel to members as needed. This person would also travel with the ministry team whenever possible. The Chaplain works alongside the Director to aid in addressing spiritual matters concerning the team.

Choreographer (s): The role of the choreographer is vital to the Arts Ministry team. Whether creating dances, plays, or choreo-dramas, this individual must stay on the cutting edge of what is happening in the world NOW. The choreographer must work closely with the Director and Assistant Director in order to maintain the vision that God has set forth for the team overall. The choreographer must maintain a strong connection and balance between being led by the Holy Spirit and being relevant to the Church. The individual(s) in this role must also maintain their technical expertise in a variety of dance and theatre forms. This will assist in maintaining the integrity of their role as choreographers. This individual should also be an excellent, called, and anointed communicator and **teacher**.

Praise Garment Designer/Seamstress: It should be understood, however, as a point of reminder, the designer and/or seamstress for the Arts Ministry Team must be born-again, Spirit-filled Believers. As described in Exodus Chapter 28:2-3, the individuals must be highly skilled and full of wisdom in order to create garments that are glorious and praiseworthy to the Lord. Therefore, these individuals must also work closely with the Directors in order to capture the vision and spirit of the team. The designer and seamstress should strive to be both culturally and Kingdom-relevant in their creations. These individuals must also be familiar with the choreographic repertoire of the team. This will assist in making wise decisions regarding specific costuming, fabrics, and the like, which will enhance the ministry presentation.

Audio Engineer: This individual should be skilled and trained in various aspects of sound engineering and technology. During scheduled meeting and rehearsal times, this individual should become acquainted with all necessary aspects of the dance or dramatic ministry presentations that require sound effects or music. This person must work closely with the Directors and the Choreographers to stay abreast of the kinds and types of music required for the ministry. He or she may elect to have duplicate copies of all musical selections in the ministry's repertoire. The audio engineer should ensure proper cuing of CDs or cassettes at the appointed time of ministry. This individual should insist on timely sound checks during ministry engagements. As this role is critical to the success of the ministry team, the audio engineers must be equipped and able to take authority in the spirit realm over all manner of technical difficulties, power outages, and equipment trouble during times of ministry.

The Administrative Staff may look similar to this:

Administrative Staff:

Lead Administrator: The lead administrator is responsible for all administrative functions for the ministry team. He or she works closely with the directors to ensure that overall organization, assimilation, and distribution of information to the team is executed. Coordinates with the director administratively in regards to ministry engagements, and logistics such as transportation, accommodations, and the like. Overall, this individual serves as an administrative assistant to the director.

Marketing/Events Coordinator: The Marketing/Events Coordinator is responsible for promoting the ministry team in a godly and excellent fashion throughout the community and the city locally or abroad. He or she should seek out opportunities to minister in various arenas and venues. The coordinator should keep the team abreast of other ministry functions, seminars, conferences, and the like.

**(For Those Who Direct a Children's Dance Ministry) Parent's Core: This team of parents assist in the general welfare of the younger children outside of the classroom. They assist in rallying other parents for outside activities and fundraisers, including the recruitment of other potential children into the teaching ministry. The parents core would also assist in the corporate disciplinary action, if needed, for their own children.

Finance Administrator: The Financial Administrator establishes and maintains accounting records for the team through banking and excellent stewardship. He or she ensures proper procedures are maintained with regards to intake and distribution, seeks out opportunities to invest in other ministries and charitable organizations, and pays all ministry team bills/obligations. The Financial Administrator must also ensure that the ministry team pays a regular tithe to the church under which they are covered.

Fundraising Representatives: The Fundraising Coordinator plans and supervises activities and events that will serve to bring in and generate income to the ministry team's general fund. From the initial concept to its completion, these persons will develop creative, innovative ways to generate income for the sustaining, welfare, and advancement of the ministry.

The administration of any successful ministry must be handled professionally, with good ethics. The administration of a ministry should be managed with even more zeal and excellence than that of any secular organization. Depending upon the size of your ministry team, all of the above-mentioned positions may not be necessary. However, in the planning stages, it is always good to have established guidelines. We should view this administrative position of the Arts Ministry as our 'worship' offered unto God as well. Remembering just as Paul admonished the church at Corinth in 1Corinthians 14:40 that with all the prophesies, tongues, and moves of the spirit that were going forth, the Lord would still require that everything be done in a decent, fitting, and orderly way. If sacred artists and ministers follow this guiding principle, the heart of the Father will be blessed and glory will be brought to His name.

Prayer Declaration:

God I praise You for Your Excellency!
I declare that from this day forward, I will no longer
settle for mediocrity in ministry;
I thank You for Creating me in Your own image
and likeness, Lord;
Now help me to see myself as You see me;
Thank You God for delivering me from a spirit of
confusion and chaos, and for now
Bringing me into supernatural structure and focus
with ROOM to Breathe!
In Jesus' Name,
AMEN.

Reader's Reflections:

(Fill in your own personal statements of affirmation.)

My Affirmations:

One area of my life requiring order is _____

_____

_____

Administratively, I must _____

_____

_____

I will take the first step by _____

_____

_____

_____

_____

_____

Sacred AFFIRMATION #9

**I CAN Soar!
I HAVE Peace!
I AM BEING Made Whole!
I BELIEVE on the Lord Jesus Christ!
I GLOW inwardly!
I GROW in the Knowledge of God!
I AWAIT transformation!**

CHAPTER NINE

The Glorious Priesthood of Sacred Artistry

"You also, like living stones, are being built into
a spiritual house to be a holy priesthood, offering spiritual sacrifices acceptable to God
through Jesus Christ." IPeter 2:5

"But you are a chosen people, a royal priesthood a holy nation, a people belonging to God,
that you may declare the praises of Him who
called you out of darkness into His wonderful
light..." IPeter 2:9

The 'glorious priesthood' in the world of Sacred Arts
refers to a holy community comprised of consecrated
artists, dramatists, musicians, minstrels, singers, psalmists,
and dance ministers. These communities of persons are
those who have received, accepted, and are acting upon
God's call on their lives to minister to Him and to His people. As sacred artists, many of us were indeed 'called out' of
the professional, secular world of performing arts, into His

wonderful light of ministry. This call is what compels the sacred artist to bring down the glory of God in all majesty, splendor and excellence of praise to the Father in *their specific area* of discipline.

In complete acceptance to this assignment, the Sacred Artist begins to live out the scripture in Romans 12:1-2 that says:

> **"I urge you, in view of God's mercy, that you present your bodies as living sacrifices, holy and acceptable to God—this is your spiritual act of worship. And do not be conformed to this world, but be transformed by the renewing of your mind..."**

This is a process. For many Sacred Artists, this renewing of the mind will initially consist of an inner cleansing and washing with the Word and with personal revelations from God. As the Holy Spirit matures and teaches us, this mind renewal will change from an inward expression to an outward manifestation similar to that of which Jabez prayed to God in 1Chronicles 4:10: "Oh, that you would bless me indeed and that you would enlarge my territory". As the minister yields in submission, the Lord answers their prayer. He enlarges the sacred artist's territory, as well as his or her vision and revelation for how their own gifting may be interwoven in the plans and purposes of the Father.

Strategically, God moves and places persons throughout the Nations for the purpose of occupying, seizing, and possessing the land for His Kingdom. For example, when the Spirit of God sends us to a particular territory of the world, it is an indication that He is vitally concerned about the people of that land. More so, He desires that a particular group of people receives specific discipleship and training from His sent servant, the Sacred Arts Minister.

When Jesus commanded us to "go into all the worlds and preach the Gospel" He never specified the manner in which we are to go. It is only clear that we must go. Unfortunately, over time, man has placed many restrictions on this concept of preaching and has attempted to stifle a dynamic and creative God to using verbal articulation only. What could be the theological justification for this? Some use Romans 10:14, saying that "Faith cometh by hearing, and hearing by the Word of God." Furthermore, the scriptures go on to ask the question, "How can they hear unless a preacher preaches...?" Still others proclaim that in order to be effective in evangelism, one must convince and convict lost souls from sin through the spoken word. Does this then mean that the entire population of deaf and dumb individuals are on their way to hell because they did not receive Christ through hearing the Word? What about the countless number of people who refuse to set foot in a church building, but may happen to stop at a Town Square or stadium where a dance or drama production is being ministered? If what they see with their eyes touches their hearts, and they give their lives to Christ, are they destined for hell because they came to Christ through a dance? After all, the final words of Romans 10:15 says, "How beautiful are the feet of those who bring the Good News!" Jesus left **how** we are to go into the world open to our own creative interpretation. Therefore, when it comes to training and discipling the World, we must identify our individual areas of calling and expertise which may be all-inclusive of preaching, teaching, evangelizing, and prophesying the Word of God in various forms and expressions of sacred artistry. As an ordained minister of the Gospel, I am by no means de-emphasizing the power and absolute necessity of the spoken, preached Word. I am stating, however that there are times when the message God gives me to preach may call for a "full-body expression" in which words will just not do. One must yield to the prompting of the Holy Spirit by utilizing whichever gift necessary for that particular ministry experience.

Levitical and Priestly Implications: Then and Now

Individuals whom God has chosen to train and prepare as His present-day Levitical priesthood have a tremendous responsibility to uphold and are inevitably called to leadership. Since the days of Moses and Aaron, the Levites served and ministered unto the Lord. Originally, the Levites were those solely consecrated to carry the tabernacle and care for all articles used in its service. Later, King David declared that this service would no longer be necessary since the LORD, the God of Israel granted rest to his people, and came to dwell in Jerusalem forever. This indwelling was to occur in the Temple that Solomon, son of David would build. From that time, the duty of the Levites was to help Aaron's descendants in the service of the temple of the LORD. This included: to be in charge of the courtyards, the side rooms, the purification of all sacred things, and the performance of other duties at the House of God. They were in charge of the bread, the flour for the grain offerings, the unleavened wafers, the baking and mixing, and all measurements of quantity and size. In addition, 1Chronicles 23:30 also cites:

> **"The Levites were also to stand every morning to thank and praise the LORD. They were to do the same in the evening, and whenever burnt offerings were presented to the LORD on Sabbaths and at New Moon festivals and at appointed feasts."**

While their primary responsibility was to minister unto the LORD, the Levites also taught and trained the people in issues of morality and religion. Many theologians believe that the Levites worked with the Prophets, and were actually trained by them. This interaction with the prophets of God may explain some of the personality traits of a true Levite, which may be described as passionate, uncompromising, and sometimes ruthless in all matters relating to their Covenant with God. Moses said of Levi prior to his death in Deuteronomy 33:9-11:

> **"He said of his father and mother, 'I have no regard for them.' He did not recognize his brothers or acknowledge his own children, but he watched over your word and guarded your covenant. He teaches your precepts to Jacob and your law to Israel. He offers incense before you and whole burnt offerings on your altar. Bless all his skills, O LORD, and be pleased with the work of his hands. Smite the loins of those who rise up against him; strike his foes till they rise no more."**

Moses knew the ferocity with which Levi would keep watch over the Covenant. He observed and lived among each of the tribes for years and knew their strengths, weaknesses, and sincerity of heart. Of Levi, Moses also knew of their most excellent teachings and offerings unto the Lord. He mentions Levi making offerings of *incense*. The altar for the offering of incense was symbolic of *continuous intercession* before the Lord, and these prayers were to last throughout generations to come (Ex. 30:1-10).

Moses' statements concerning Levi were not to imply that they were cold and uncaring about their families, however, to make known that the Levites were trained to have no regard for anyone or anything involved in the dishonor or desecration of the holiness of God. As we examine ourselves as ministers today, how many of us would pass this test? While one may long to be used of God in this capacity, the individual's life and convictions must measure up to the Lord's standard. Many of us are involved in situations concerning family, friends, church members and co-workers that we know to be ungodly, yet, are either too afraid or unwilling to confront it. This is not the nature of a Levite. The 21st Century Levite must be willing and able to address dysfunction within their own house first, then in the House of God, and society by using the weapons of a consecrated lifestyle, praise, and spiritual warfare. Indeed, the Father is seeking individuals who understand that their lives are in His hands, therefore, no amount of adversity will deter God's servant from speaking and exacting justice when it is in their power to do so. This is the true heritage of the prophet and the Levite.

Ministry Unto God

Consider the words found in Exodus 28:1-1-3:

> **"From among the Israelites, take your brother Aaron and his sons with him, that he may minister to Me in the priest's office, even Aaron, Nadab, and Abihu, Eleazar and Ithamar, Aaron's sons. And you shall make for Aaron your brother sacred garments for honor and beauty. Tell all who are expert, whom I have endowed with skill and good judgement, that they shall make Aaron's garments to sanctify him for My priesthood." (Amplified)**

God is very particular about the ministry we bring to Him. As the scriptures show, He was so particular about who would minister to Him, where they would minister, how they would minister, and even in what kind of attire they would minister in—so much so that He gave detailed, meticulous instructions for the priests to follow. The excellence of the ministry offered unto the Lord must not be taken for granted. Our ministry to Him can either be offered as a 'sweet smelling savor' or as a 'stench' in the Father's nostrils.

As a minister of sacred arts in His glorious priesthood, our number one assignment is to minister to God the Father FIRST—not to an audience or a congregation. As long as this is kept in perspective, one can all but eliminate the temptation of 'performing' in the flesh under the guise of 'ministry' to the Lord. Staying in tuned with the Holy Spirit of God will reveal what the Father wants, and how He wants it. This should be the premiere objective of our ministry. The Father is seeking *true* worshippers who will honor Him in Spirit and in Truth. It is these individuals who are not afraid to change a planned ministry presentation at the last minute—whether it be in song, message, or a particular piece of choreography—all because the Holy Spirit announces the Father's will to go in a totally different direction! Seizing moments like this are but another hurdle towards true obedience, and the ability to clear this hurdle will always bring us into a new realm of intimacy through worship and relationship with God.

When God empowers the sacred artist in the MINISTRY of the Glorious Priesthood, it gives them the authority to evoke CHANGE in the atmosphere.

Preparing the Way

> **"The word of the LORD came to Jeremiah: "This is what the LORD says: 'If you can break my covenant with the day and my covenant with the night, so that day and night no longer come at their appointed time, then my covenant with David my servant—and my covenant with the Levites who are priests ministering before me—can be broken and David**

will no longer have a descendant to reign on his throne. I will make the descendants of David my servant and the Levites who minister before me as countless as the stars of the sky and as measureless as the sand on the seashore'".
Jeremiah 33:19-22

What an incredible promise God makes to the descendants of the Levites! He desires to have countless numbers of Levites whom He knows will uphold His standard of holiness in the Earth. Notice how God makes His covenant with those Levites who *minister before Him!* The 21st Century Minister of Arts plays a vital role in fulfillment of this prophecy as he or she consecrates their gift of song, music, dance, drama, art, and their very lives to God and His Kingdom.

Revelation:

Keep doing what is natural until you run into the *Supernatural.*

—Dr. Cecelia Williams Bryant, Texas, USA
October 1999

Truly the practitioner of sacred artistry has been called into the Kingdom for such a time as this! There is a sense of urgency in the spirit realm to bring as many lost souls to the knowledge of Jesus Christ as possible. One needs only to look at television, radio, movies and other secular art forms to see that our society has become plagued with witchcraft, sorcery, perversion, and violence. The devil has seemingly pulled out all the stops and has unleashed wickedness and evil of unimaginable proportions. Children's video games have become murderous and sexual in content and nature. Children's books offer precise detail on how to become wizards, control minds, and obtain power over others. If the music videos are not showing graphic and provocative sex scenes, they are showing unbridled homosexuality, Satanism, cultist, ghosts that torture while singing a hip tune, and gruesome depictions of the resurrection of the dead. Many of our churches have lost their vision to overdone commercialism, networking, and strife.

Yet, in all of this, the Lord God Jehovah remains Sovereign. All these things must manifest so that the End may come. The ministers of the Glorious Priesthood have a vital role to play in these times. God reminds us that it is the Levites who will prepare the way for the New Kingdom and the coming of Christ. It is our responsibility to set the atmosphere, prepare the hearts of the people, and lay the foundational groundwork for the Kingdom of God here on earth:

"See, I will send my messenger who will prepare the way before me. Then suddenly the Lord you are seeking will come to his temple; the messenger of the covenant, whom you desire, will come," says the Lord Almighty. But who can endure the day of his coming? Who can stand when he appears? For he will be like a refiner's fire or a launderer's soap. He will sit as a refiner and purifier of silver; he will purify the Levites and refine them like gold and silver. Then the Lord will have men who are able to bring offerings in righteousness and the offerings of Judah and Jerusalem will be acceptable to the LORD, as in days gone by as in the former years. So, I will come near to you for judgment. I will be quick to testify against sorcerers, adulterers and perjurers, against those who

defraud laborers of their wages, who oppress the widows and the fatherless, and deprive aliens of justice, but do not fear me," says the LORD Almighty. (Malachi 3:1-5)

The Glorious Priesthood of Levitical psalmists, musicians, dancers, poets, dramatists, and writers must position themselves to be used of God prophetically and supernaturally in this season. They must be willing to go into 'all worlds', ministering to God first, and then to His hurting people. Many of the ideas and venues that the Holy Spirit proposes for ministry may seem unconventional, uncouth, and at times impossible. But remember, these same Levites must **themselves first** be prepared in order to prepare the way for the King of Kings.

It is the sacred artist's responsibility to obtain the proper training and teaching in order to fulfil their calling into this ministry. The individual must delve deeply into the Word of God. He or she must also seek out institutions and programs that offer excellent curriculum in their field. Just as the biblical Levites worked and trained with the school of the Prophets, so too should today's Levites. Submission to a Word-based Pastor, Bishop, Apostle, or *credible* Prophet will be key in the shaping of the individual's 'kingdom', 'nation', and 'missions' mind-sets and frames of reference.

But now, where is His Temple as prophesied in Malachi 3:1? Where is this Holy Dwelling place that the LORD Almighty longs to come into? Where is this Sanctuary that can withstand the Refiner's fire, and what kind of Awesome Wonder is this Temple anyway? So Majestic that even the Prophet Zechariah declares that a crown will be dedicated within its walls and it will draw people from afar? What? Know ye not that Your Body IS the Temple of the Holy Spirit that is in you and that you are not your own! YOU are the 'New Thing' that God is doing! You have been bought with a price, therefore being woven into the fibers of the Branch, that is Christ Jesus. Therefore, because you are the Offspring of Christ, then shall the offspring of your own Temple also be destined for this Glorious Priesthood! The Book of Acts 17:28-29 declares:

> **"The God who made the world and everything in it is the Lord of heaven and earth and does not live in temples built by hands. And, he is not served by human hands, as if he needed anything, because he himself gives all men life and breath and everything else. From one man he made every nation of men, that they should inhabit the whole earth; and he determined the times set for them and the exact places where they should live. God did this so that men would seek him and find him, though he is not far from each one of us. For in him, we live, and move, and have our being. As some of your poets have said, 'We are his offspring.'"**

Human hands do not serve God; rather, he is *ministered to* with our spirits as we keep our Body-Temples ALIVE. The sacred arts minister MUST move—it is how we SURVIVE! More importantly, it is how we perpetuate our seed. There must be an understanding of legacy, succession, and moving from glory to glory for generations to come. God must receive a return on His investment in each of us, and His investment in us is primarily due to what He knows is inside of us—our seed!

Envisioning Your Seed

One Sunday evening, my spiritual godmother, Dr. Patricia Morgan, spoke very passionately about caring for the children of the nations and how we must develop a heart of compassion for them. Although I had heard her speak on this topic many times before, there was a special anointing on the words she spoke to the audience that night. When I closed my eyes, the Lord gave me a prophetic vision. It was of my daughter-to-be! She was so beautiful and looked to be about one year old. She sat on top of an embroidered white pillow and she wore a simple white cotton dress—her eyes were wide and bright; dark brown, with very long eyelashes; and of all things, she was LAUGHING at me! Just then, she took up a tiny flask of oil and poured a few drops in the palms of her hands. She rubbed them together, and with a loud, joyous shout, lifted her hands high in the air! When I opened my eyes, tears were streaming down my face as the voice of the Holy Spirit confirmed that my daughter, who has not yet been born to me, will be a Healer! That night, I slept so peacefully. When I woke up the next morning, the Lord sent me straight to 1Chronicles 17:4. My mind could hardly believe what my eyes were reading:

"You are not the one who will build a house for me to dwell in. I have not dwelt in a house from the day I brought Israel up out of Egypt to this day. I have moved from one tent site to another, and from one dwelling place to another. Wherever I moved, did I ever say to any of their leaders, "Why have you not built me a house of cedar?" ...Now then, tell my servant David, this is what the Lord Almighty says: I took you from the pasture and from following the flock, to be ruler over my people Israel. I have been with you wherever you have gone, and I have cut off all your enemies from before you. Now I will make your name like the names of the greatest men on earth. I will provide a place for my people Israel and will plant them

so that they can have a home of their own and no longer be disturbed...Wicked people will not oppress them anymore, as they did at the beginning, and have done ever since the time I appointed leaders over my people, Israel. I will also subdue all of your enemies. I will declare to you that the LORD Himself will build a house for you. When your days are over and you go to be with your fathers, I will raise up your offspring to succeed; one of your own sons, and I will establish his kingdom. He is the one that will build a house for me and I will establish his throne forever."

Why is this incident so significant? Because although originally, God gave this promise to King David and his son Solomon, I am able to receive this promise for my own off-spring and for me! God always confirms the vision He gives to His servants with His Word. Has God given *you* a dream or vision of the New Millennium 'Kingdom Children'? If so, how far are you willing to go in your Christian walk to see it come to fruition?

Revelation:
It's one thing to believe. It's another to ACT on what you believe through CHANGE and TRANSFORMATION.

Our responsibility as leaders in the Glorious Priesthood extends to the current generation, tomorrow's generation, and to our daughters and sons who have not yet been formed in the womb. Our successful impartation to those whom we can directly affect NOW will determine the level of fulfill-

ment of God's prophetic promises for us. This is why every
<u>true</u> leader will also be a mentor. We must commit to living
and demonstrating a consecrated life before God and in the
eyes of His people. When this is done successfully, one will
be quick to discern and disciple persons who are destined
for greatness and leadership in the Glorious Priesthood of
Sacred Arts. The sacred arts minister will then graduate
from technician, teacher, and trainer, into the shoes of an
Arts Ambassador with apostolic gifting and ability to provide a new dimension of leadership, consultation, and discipleship to the entire Arts world.

The Arts world will have territorial facets that will either
be spiritual or geographical in nature. As the Lord commis-
sions the individual into the nations, He reveals and assigns
them to the designated land(s) that He desires to be conquered and possessed for the Kingdom. One must know that
God does not call an individual to love and serve the 'land',
rather, He calls them to love the **people** of the land. This is
one common stumbling block that many missionaries have
fallen over. They may have understood and answered the
call, but they have an unrealistic, self-serving, and pious perception of "what's in it for them". Love of the physical land
itself, with no sincere regard for the people, will most cer-
tainly be their downfall. Satan will detect this characteristic
from its inception and will attempt to use it for destruction.
It is crucial that upon commissioning, the individual boldly
and confidently accepts their territorial mission/assignment
because in the realm of spiritual warfare, rest assured that
there will be territorial demons and strongholds assigned to
sabotage and destroy God's intended plan.

<u>Prayer Declaration:</u>

Dear Lord,
I believe that You are in control of my life;
I ask You now, Father to reveal and confirm
Your calling on my life;
If YOU ASK of me, I WILL answer; but Lord please help
me to flow according to Your timing—not mine;
I trust You for the outcome that You desire;
I align my will again WITH Yours;
I prepare myself psychologically, spiritually, and
emotionally to MOVE into the next GLORIOUS
Phase of Priestly Service, Ministry, and Warfare;
Blessed be the Name of Jesus!
AMEN.

Reader's Reflections:

(Fill in your own personal statements of affirmation.)

My Affirmations:

I must purge my mind of _____
in order to flow in the glorious priesthood.

I believe that I am called to the nation(s) of _____

_____

My greatest challenge in the preparation process is

_____

_____

I will overcome this challenge by _____

_____

_____

<u>Sacred AFFIRMATION #10</u>

I HAVE Authority Over the Enemy!

I WILL Dance in Opposition to the Rulers of Darkness!

MY Weapons of Praise Far Outweigh Satan's Tactics of Intimidation!

I GIVE Myself Over to Becoming the LORD's Battleaxe!

CHAPTER TEN

WAR Dance!

"And I have commanded my holy ones; I have summoned my warriors to carry out my wrath- those who will rejoice in my triumph. Listen, a noise on the mountains, like that of a great multitude! Listen, uproar among the kingdoms like nations massing together! The LORD Almighty is mustering an army for war!" (Isaiah 13:3-4)

In a Dream recorded from the author's journal in 1997:
I beheld a beautiful garden. It was full of many flowers of many colors. It was so lush and radiant with the light of the sun. There was a small path clearly shown down the middle of the garden. From behind one of the tall bushes, I appeared, dressed in my dance garments: they were full white, trimmed in gold, and topped off by an ephod of the 12 tribes of Judah. As I walked slowly down the path, I stopped for a moment to lift my hands in praise to God. All at once, a long, silver sword was placed in my right hand! I heard what I believed to be the Voice of the Lord directing

me saying, "Daughter, hold the sword outright and steady." I obeyed, advancing forward on the path, deeper and deeper into the garden.

When I awoke from this dream the next morning, lying in my bed, the Holy Spirit of God directed me to open my Bible to Psalm 18. My eyes fell upon verses 32 and beyond which said:

> **"It is God who arms me with strength and makes my way perfect. He makes my feet like the feet of a deer; he enables me to stand on the heights. He trains my hands for battle; my arms can bend a bow of bronze. You give me your shield of victory, and your right hand sustains me; you stoop down to make me great. You broaden the path beneath me, so that my ankles do not turn. I pursued my enemies and overtook them; I did not turn back till they were destroyed."**

This encounter with God began my official commissioning to *intentionally utilize* the ministry of dance in spiritual warfare. As the dream indicated, I was to walk in His path and uphold the standard of holiness "outright and steady", eliminating anything that would try to come against it. This was also the year in which I completely accepted the call to full-time ministry of the Word. Up until this point, much of my teaching to others was with regards to technique, worship, holiness, liturgy, and healing through movement. However in my own personal life, I was experiencing some of the most violent attacks from the enemy against my mind, my self-esteem, and my physical body. These attacks frequently manifested themselves in dreams and visions—all of which I kept detailed recordings of in my journals. With the help of the Holy Spirit, I determined that God desired to have a 'teaching moment' with me. He began to reveal the method of deliverance He wanted me to follow. I began to study my journals intensely, alongside of the Word of God. Soon, I was able to identify which of these documented dreams were from God, and which were not. I noticed the pattern and frequency of the enemy's affronts towards me. They were:

- During times of great personal achievement or acknowledgement in my work or ministry
- Whenever I was on the verge of a spiritual breakthrough
- Immediately following a ministry engagement or seminar
- Any attempt I made to become debt-free and more financially stable
- During times of deepened commitment in a personal relationship

No amount of prayer, intercession, speaking in tongues, laying on of hands, or anointing oil assisted in freeing me from this oppression. Not to mention that most ministers of the Gospel of whom I sought counsel were not only ineffective, but were unwilling to BELIEVE and acknowledge that I was, in fact 'warring' in my dreams! I decided to stop talking, and start dancing the Dance of WAR. It became my *personal vendetta* against the devil. During this season, there were times (and still are) when, in the middle of the night, the Holy Spirit would prompt me to WAR. While my previous understanding of this 'call' had been to get up and intercede by praying in the Spirit, my new mode of intercession became the Dance of War! This would prove to be the Way to my deliverance.

The common understanding of war throughout the scriptures refers to a state of hostility and irreconcilable conflict between nations, states, provinces, or parties of individuals. This hostility can prove to be both spiritual and physical in nature. Biblically, there were two kinds of war recognized.

The first was **obligatory** in nature, that is, being expressly commanded by the Lord. These wars that were undertaken at the direction of God always proved victorious, as He assured those whom He had commanded that He would be with them. The second type of war was **voluntary** and free in nature. These wars were engaged in at the direction of man— usually leaders, kings, or captains of a people for the purpose of personal or national revenge, punishment of an insult or assault, or to maintain power. As a point of reference, it is this later form of war that the United States has declared on world-wide terrorism—this as a result of the violent and deadly attacks on America on September 11, 2001.

As one moves through each facet of knowledge and understanding regarding the ministry of dance artistry, it is in this season that the sacred minister must sharpen his or her sword. In doing so, we fully prepare our Body-Temples not only for worship, but also for the Dance of WAR.

Therefore, now, with the power and authority vested in me through the Lord Jesus Christ, I command you: "Daughters and Sons of the Most High God, Arise!; Ministers of the Glorious Priesthood—Draw your swords into your right hand, hold them outright and steady; **CHARGE!**"

The Defense

The hostility between humankind and satan has shifted back and forth throughout the years. However, the intense disdain and hatred between the **woman** and satan was prophesied from the Beginning as a result of The Fall of mankind. God declared to satan in Genesis 3:15:

> **"And I will put enmity between you and the woman, and between your offspring and hers; he will *crush* your head, and you will *strike* his heel."**

No one can deny the vital role that the woman must play in spiritual warfare. God could have commanded any other fate to fall upon the woman as a result of Eve's actions, but instead, He simply called her to eternal WAR with the enemy—that is, to hate that which is evil. The woman is a born survivor. She possesses the Spirit of the Warrior because the Lord equipped her as such. Women should never deny nor defend their instincts to fight against injustice as it pertains to the Kingdom, the family, and the communities in which they live. However, one must be wise in choosing only those battles assigned to her according to the purposes of God. The woman's enmity is ***not*** with the man. To be clear, it is with satan.

Usually, in order to 'strike' at anything with precision, one must get very **close. This** is a natural gifting of a woman in worship—by and large, it is the woman who will plunge herself into the worship experience with reckless abandon for the King of Kings. As the sincere worshiper is led beyond the veil, the Holy Spirit of God begins to reveal and uncover many things. In the case of the arts minister, the revelations may even uncover a hidden truth: that they have been dancing ***with*** the enemy. It is the supernatural favor of God which affords us the grace to 'flush out' the enemy from our midst. As stated earlier, we must study and know our opponent *intimately* so that when we do strike, the hit is sure and devastating.

The **godly man** who ministers in sacred dance has the ability to bring forth a double blow to the kingdom of darkness. Not only does he maintain his leadership role as king, priest, and warrior, but as a man of God, he's been given the authority to call forth 'Death' to that which has been struck by the woman! Men and women in ministry together must acknowledge, accept, and respect the prescribed roles assigned to each of them by God from the Beginning. There is power in agreement! As the scriptures say, "One can chase a thousand, but two can put ten thousand to flight..." Yes, together as men and women of God, we will do great exploits!

Power in the Feet

The Lord foretold that the WAR which would rage from now until the end of time, would not be won solely through speaking prophetic declarations over our nations, but through ACTIVE use of our bodies—in particular, through the use of our **feet**. The human foot is one of God's most amazing creations. Our feet serve as shock absorbers for the entire body. Doctors say that the feet can cushion up to one million pounds of pressure during just an hour of strenuous exercise! The strongest and largest tendon in the human body is the Achilles tendon. This tendon connects the calf muscles to the **heel** of the foot. This is why God's promise of satan's impending doom is so powerful—when we, the offspring of Christ, and our own offspring, come together to *strike* satan's heel, we utilize the power of the heel to destroy him and cut him down! He then comes under our authority through Jesus Christ, who proclaimed that He himself has placed all things 'under His feet'.

While theologians and Believers alike may find this premise utterly ridiculous, there is scriptural support that describes the true warrior's call to use one's body militantly in 'active duty' as the battle for the souls of nations continues:

> "The weapons of our warfare are not of this world, but are mighty through God to the **pulling down** of strongholds." (2Cor. 10:4)

> "We **wrestle** not against flesh and blood, but against powers, rulers, and spiritual wickedness in High Places." (Ephesians 6:12)

"Or again, how can anyone **enter** a strong man's house and **carry** off his possessions unless he first **ties up** the strong man?" (Matthew 12:29)

"I will give you the keys of the kingdom of heaven; whatever you **bind** on earth will be **bound** in heaven, and whatever you **loose** on earth will be **loosed** in heaven." (Matthew 16:19)

"**Come here** and **put your feet** on the necks of these kings." So they came forward and placed their feet on their necks. Joshua said to them, "Do not be afraid; do not be discouraged. This is what the LORD will do to all the enemies you are going to fight." (Joshua 10:24)

"On that day, Moses swore to me, 'The land on which your **feet have walked** will be your inheritance and that of your children forever, because you have **followed** the LORD my God wholeheartedly." (Joshua 14:9)

"Then you will **trample down** the wicked; they will be ashes under the soles of **your feet** on the day when I do these things, says the LORD Almighty." (Malachi 4:3)

"For he must reign until he has **put** all his enemies **under his feet**. The last enemy to be destroyed in death." (1Corinthians 15:25-26)

"The God of Peace will soon **crush** satan **under your feet**." (Romans 16:20)

"Stand firm then, with the belt of truth buckled

around your waist, with the breastplate of righteousness in place, and with your **feet fitted** with the readiness that comes from the gospel of peace." (Ephesians 6:14-15)

Revelation:
You must engage yourself into the life of your community through active, violent, INTERVENTION against the enemy.

—*Dr. Patricia Morgan, South Africa*
August 2000

The Sacred Arts community is rising to the forefront of society with the anointing and ability to transform a world of evil. While many of our politicians, lawmakers, and government officials succumb to a corrupt society, it is the artistic military forces of the Most High God who are shaking the earth with the Spirit of PRAISE! Contrary to popular belief, our battle is NOT just in spiritual warfare. While at the root of every conflict there may be an underlying spiritual issue at work, there will be times of intense PHYSICAL fighting that must take place. Ecclesiastes 3:8-9 reminds us that there is, "a time to love and a time to hate; a time for war and a time for peace." With the state of the World as it is today, no one can truly say that there is peace. Peace will come, but not without a fight!

Oftentimes, God the Father will allow what seem to be catastrophic circumstances to befall us. *Repeatedly!* And while we appear to be losing our minds and wondering, "WHY me?", the Holy Spirit of God is mustering up His army. He must bring us to the point that we declare to satan that we are 'mad as hell, and not going to take it anymore!'

God has ALREADY equipped us. We have His Word, we have our Body-Temples, and we have each other—He is not giving us anything else to fight with! The WAR must be danced in unity and this must be embraced as an intrinsic truth among the community of sacred artists.

Search, Kill, and Destroy: WAR Dance Strategies

Do you realize how much the devil hates you? Do you realize how much the devil studies you? He seeks you out no matter where you are. Don't be deceived. After all, you, as a sacred artist, are now occupying a position once held by him—Lucifer, (satan) was the original worship leader. Therefore, not only does he long for you to turn to *him,* but also, he longs to control and manipulate your gift and that of the entire Arts world. It is the job of a good enemy to know their opponents intimately—how else may one determine their strengths and weaknesses? The primary strategy in opposing the enemy comes through WAR Dances based on the principle found in James 4:7 that states, "Submit yourselves to God. Resist the devil and he will flee." Personal obedience and discipline to the Lord will determine the strength of your resistance efforts. So, you think you're a priest. Maybe so. But can you fight? Remember, the tribe of Levi found favor with God and Moses because of the ferocity with which they protected the holy things of God! Consider the three following strategies in the Dance of War: **Search, Kill, and Destroy:**

Strategy #1: SEARCH for Resistance

The Hebrew translation for 'resist' means to provoke; to rebel; to make bitter; to disobey and accuse; to attack and to be an adversary to! In the original Greek translation, 'resist' means 'to stand in opposition'. What trouble the kingdom of darkness faces on the Day when true worshippers demonstrate an all out "Resistance Campaign" *against* the devil instead of running away from him! Just as the devil 'seeks' those whom he may devour, the sacred artist must make a conscious decision to seek after evil at every turn. One problem for some ministries today is that they are entering into *worship* without acknowledging the need for WARfare. Some are too afraid of the repercussions that may come through on-lookers and even some pastors who may place stereotypes upon them that they are too wild, resemble voodoo and witchcraft, and are out of control. When warfare is called for under the precise direction of the Holy Spirit, nothing could be farther from the truth. The discerning worshiper will recognize this immediately. Other timid Believers refrain from entering into warfare for fear of repercussions from the devil himself. These fears must not stifle the warrior from *moving* in accordance to the Spirit. The WAR Dances are bold steps of FAITH. One's *resistance* in this war can no longer be an attempt to withdraw or abstain. The Call to War is one that pushes us from comfort and passivity to ACTIVE AGGRESSION. It is accomplished when the warrior's body intercedes prophetically, in an attitude of holy violence, outrage, disgust, contempt, aggression, and all-out hatred aimed at satan which reaches that of fanatical proportions!

Revelation:

The relevance of your ministry must be *Revolutionary*. You must be the kind of Christian who will turn the WORLD upside down!

—Dr. Peter Morgan, Jamaica
September 2001

Strategy #2: KILL Or Be Killed

Have you ever seen the Zulu Warriors both *before* and *during* a battle? They are ruthless in their preparations as well as in their fighting. Just as the soldiers of the Old Testament oftentimes engaged in ceremonial marches before they fought, the Zulu Warriors engage in ceremonial War Dance maneuvers. As they stir up their zeal through high-energy, intense, and aggressive movements, they prepare themselves mentally and physically for 'the kill'. Physically, the warrior's muscles flex as an outward boast to the opponent of their impending death. Inwardly, the warrior must kill *self*. Sacred dance warriors put their wills, desires, passions, and motives at the foot of the Cross. Whether it be to stretch out, laying prostrate on the floor, or to dance oneself into complete submission until your Body-Temple is exhausted, the inward death must have its time. This is what Paul means when he says in 1Corinthians 9:27, "No, I beat my body and make it a slave so that after I have preached to others, I myself will not be disqualified for the prize." Later in 1Corinthians 15:31, he speaks of "dying daily" to the flesh. Unless one dies to self, the enemy will surely overtake their soul. Therefore, the first death that must occur is *our own*.

With our own spiritual death settled, the Spirit of God allows the true warrior to be resurrected in us. Now, untainted and undistracted, *we* are the aggressors—hunting our prey. The fight we fight is real, and the dance we dance is pure fire. Assaulted, victimized and oppressed for so long, we become as sons and daughters of Nimrod towards the devil and his devices. The purpose in the Kill is to set the captives free. God's sacred warriors must first *identify*, then *visualize specifically* that which must be killed—otherwise called the Target. The Targets are any acts of the sinful nature that may rise up, attempting to exalt themselves against the knowledge of God. These targets may manifest through circumstances in relationships, society, the Church, or a nation. Regardless of the vessel(s) the enemy attempts to use, God has clearly listed our targets for us in Galatians 5:19-21:

- **Sexual Immorality**
- **Impurity**
- **Debauchery**
- **Idolatry**
- **Witchcraft**
- **Hatred**
- **Discord**
- **Jealousy**
- **Fits of Rage**
- **Selfish Ambition**
- **Dissension**
- **Factions**
- **Envy**
- **Drunkenness**
- **Orgies**
- **And the Like, (any related area!)**

Do not give satan the opportunity to use these acts against you, your family, nor your ministry. The sacred dance warrior remains VIGILANT in their observations, keeping a watchful eye over the things of God. Once evil is detected, there is no room for compromise.

In WAR Dance strategies, the *Search* positions the Body-Temple for resistance through prayer and prophetic intercession. The *Kill* is the action of the warrior's body that must follow.

The following is a compilation of some of the specific words that the Spirit of God spoke to me concerning His mandates and summoning to warfare in this new millennium. Has the Lord been speaking to you as well concerning this militant urgency to wage war in the heavenlies and here on earth?

A Word received from the Lord January 11, 2000:
"If you decide not to do what I have called you to do, I will make you a slave to those whom you should have been reaching in My Name."

A Word received from the Lord August 13, 2000:
"DO THE WORK! Work the Word—No time to waste! Work the Word!"

A Word received from the Lord August 13, 2000:
"Assess! Establish! Transform yourself first—then the Nations! I will use you as a Chameleon to conquer and bring reconciliation."

A Word received from the Lord October 25, 2000:
"Run for your life! Run with purpose in each step. Don't be like the boxer who misses the punches; Discipline your body like an athlete; Train it to do that which it should do."

A Word received from the Lord September 1, 2001:
"Watch Me! Do as I do—See, I stretch out My wings strong and wide! My wings shelter thousands; My wings are a refuge to many; My wings are royal and they will war."

A Word received from the Lord October 3, 2001:
"Prepare yourself! Prepare yourself for the Lamb is coming! Rejoice and be glad, all you righteous nations. Prepare yourself, for indeed I am coming soon. On the Nations, I will execute judgement; But rejoice and be glad for your Lamb is coming."

A Word received from the Lord December 31, 2001:
"Truly the Lord has called you as His warrior; Indeed God is your Man-of-War...Watch Him FIGHT for you!"

Strategy #3: DESTROY

To *destroy* is the final strategy in the WAR Dance. It is the final step to 'coming out'. For the sacred dance warrior, our final acts of destruction are found through all-out celebration before our defeated foe! We push ourselves beyond the pain and ugliness of war and assess the casualties. As our 'Targets' lie still and lifeless, the LORD of Hosts signals His warriors to utterly destroy the remains! And His choice method of demolition is through **radical praise**! This is unlike any praise that one will ever experience. In essence, the Spirit of Praise takes on a life of its own as the people of God rejoice *over* their enemies. The dancing, jumping, leaping, stomping, and RUNNING FEET of the warrior have been transformed in the spirit realm to red, hot coals—burning the Targets to ashes!

When the LORD calls for destruction through radical celebration, it must be strictly adhered to, and not quenched before its time. There may be a season of destruction that lasts for an hour, a day, or even a week—the Holy Spirit will direct; the people must simply follow. Some mighty tools of destruction used by the sacred dance warrior in order to lead the people through this final phase of warfare are African Praise, Tambourine Dances, Baton and Banner Dances, and Messianic Praise. During this season, there must also be a time when the men of God are prompted to lead in the WAR Dance. The testimonies in the lives of Bishops, Pastors, and other men of God who declare that they were totally liberated and set free from deep spiritual bondage as a result of their expressions in warfare are tremendous!

The close of a glorious season of destruction may be done

effectively through a time of reflection, thanksgiving, prophetic declarations, blessings, and CHANGE. The participants may confess verbally that which God has called them to change in their life situations, or they may simply begin to walk in it, as displayed by the attitude of their hearts. In the case of a corporate mandate which may have come from the Holy Spirit prophetically through the warfare, strategic planning teams may be called forth, ministries may be birthed and nations may be undergirded for the purpose of restoration and revitalization of a people. The WAR Dance must not leave its participants the same way as they were when it began. This change is defined as BREAK-THROUGH, and the war should not cease, until a breakthrough occurs.

As we close this chapter in prayer declarations, let us now call on the Name of the LORD by petitioning Him through His war-like characteristics:

Prayer Declaration:

Dear LORD,
Thank You for Your Call to War! LORD, we put our faith
and trust in You as we commit our bodies to dance the
dance which BINDS evil at every corner, and LOOSES
Your Spirit into the shattered areas of our lives.
We call upon you now by recognizing
that you are indeed:
Jehovah 'Oz-Lamo, The LORD,
the Strength of His People!
Jehovah Khereb, The LORD, the Sword!
Jehovah Gibbor Milchamah,
The LORD Mighty in Battle!
Jehovah Makheh, The LORD that Smiteth!
Jehovah Magen, The LORD, the Shield!
Jehovah Ma'oz, The LORD, My Fortress!
We position ourselves and declare that, "For You we Live,
and For You we will Die!" as we forcefully reclaim ALL
that the enemy has taken from us.
To Your Name be the Glory!
AMEN.

Reader's Reflections:

(Fill in your own personal statements of affirmation.)

My Affirmations:

My personal target (s) according to Galatians 5:19-22 are: _____

_____

The repercussion(s) of _____

_____

_____

will NO LONGER intimidate me.

The Word that the Spirit of God has spoken to me concerning the call to warfare is: _____

_____

_____

_____

_____

_____

Sacred AFFIRMATION #11

I AM Anointed to DREAM Dreams and SEE Visions!

I HONOR the Word of the LORD!

I HAVE Every Spiritual Gift that is Meant for Me!

I BELIEVE that My Faith in what I SEE Has the Power to HEAL Me!

I WILL Dance the Vision and MAKE it Plain!

CHAPTER ELEVEN

Prophecy and the Sacred Arts Minister

"Above all, you must understand that no prophecy of Scripture came about by the prophet's own interpretation. For prophecy never had its origin in the will of man, but men spoke from God as they were carried along by the Holy Spirit." (2Peter 1:20-21)

Why Prophesy?

The term 'to prophesy' is traditionally thought of as the act of speaking forth the Word of the Lord. Biblically, this act was usually reserved for the prophets of God. It is in this action of 'speaking forth' the heart and will of God, that the prophets actually become 'forth-tellers', that is, those who effectively bring to the forefront, and illuminate a futuristic message from the Spirit of God. The prophets who put their revelations in writing did so by divine direction from God in order that generations to come may preserve and see the fulfillment of the prophecies. As prophets speak forth the Word of God, they give themselves over completely to the will of

God by allowing their souls to be "carried along" by the Holy Spirit, as cited in 2Peter 1:20-21. Where does the Spirit carry the prophet? Supernaturally, he or she is transported into the 'IS-NESS' of God! That is, what 'is' for Him now, may not be what 'is' for us until a day to come—for with the Lord, one day is as a thousand years, and a thousand years are like a day (2Peter 3:8). So the Lord reveals to the prophet what 'is' to come, and the prophet RETURNS to the 'now' and proclaims it.

Prophetic Gift vs. the Prophetic Office

At this juncture, it is important to briefly remind the sacred arts minister that the prophetic gift one may possess, otherwise known as their 'motivational gift', is not equivalent to the office of the Prophet identified within the five-fold ministry (Ephes. 4:11). Do not be deceived into believing that because the Holy Spirit uses you prophetically at times, that this automatically makes you a Prophet or a Prophetess. There is much confusion and falsehood within the ministry of the arts among those who have boldly declared that they operate within a prophetic dance, prophetic music, or prophetic arts ministry, thus, would *now* like to be referred to as "Prophet or Prophetess X". This is absolute foolishness and will cause much pride and carnality to seep into the ministry if not addressed properly.

Romans 12:6 outlines the seven motivational gifts of the Holy Spirit: serving, teaching, exhorting, giving, leading, mercy, and ***prophesying***. These gifts help Believers to identify how they may *best flow and function* within the Body of Christ. Understanding the true spiritual 'make-up' of our brothers and sisters helps promote effectiveness, productivity, and harmony in the Body. These gifts disclose the individual's personality characteristics, or their 'modus operandi', which is being shaped and developed by the Spirit during the course of their walk with the Lord. When

submitted unto the Lordship of Jesus Christ, these characteristics now referred to as special 'gifts', afford one the
capacity to contribute to the well being and growth of themselves and others.

Conversely, in the case of what is referred to as the 5-Fold
ministry gifts found in Ephesians 4:11 (Apostle, Prophet,
Evangelist, Pastor & Teacher), we now speak more defini-
tively of a God-ordained appointment or call of an individual to a specific 'office' of service. This office is specifically
to train, equip, and prepare God's people for works of service and to build up the universal Body of Christ. This is not
to say that the minister who may possess a prophetic gifting
cannot also be called of God to the office of the Prophet.
However, we must be cautious and have the fear of the Lord
if we *place ourselves* unduly in positions of authority, and
attach undeserved or unearned titles to our ministries and
ourselves. This caution is also extended to the act of *allowing others* to attach the same to us, as a point of esteem or
reverence.

Purpose in Prophecy

There are three key motives that God has in using
prophecy. 1Corinthians 14:1-3 says, "But everyone who
prophesies speaks to men for their *strengthening, encour-
agement, and comfort.*" Therefore, the primary intent of any
word brought forth in the prophetic must meet one or all of
these criteria: to strengthen, to encourage, or to comfort. The
Holy Spirit does not set out to embarrass, or hurt the people
of God. While it is possible that in the strengthening, the
Lord may have what some refer to as a 'hard' word for the
Body or sometimes, for the individual, it is still the nature of
God to execute *judgment* with *compassion.* God is not glorified in the drudging up of past sins and personal abuses
that have no relevance to one's future. The sacred artist, who
is called into the realm of the prophetic, must long for a

supernatural encounter with Destiny—nothing more and nothing less!

Prophecy and the Musician

In the Old Testament, several references are made to the ministry of the priests and Levites who served the LORD as singers, minstrels and musicians called to prophesy on their instruments. In 1Samuel 10:5, the Bible tells of a procession of prophets who came down from the high places rejoicing, while prophesying with flutes, tambourines, and harps. In another instance, 2Kings 3:15 notes that it was the prophetic ministry of the harpist that invoked the hand of the Lord to move upon the prophet Elisha before he was able to bring forth the Word of God to King Joram of Israel and King Jehoshaphat of Judah. And in 1Chronicles 25:1, the Lord specifically instructs the sons of Asaph to be set apart for the ministry of prophesying through song and instruments. Some of these same priests and Levites are seen later in 2Chronicles 7:6 during the Dedication of the Temple that Solomon built. Through their instruments, they brought forth the prophetic praise that was interpreted as; "His love endures forever."

Any individual called by God to minister to Him as a musician must be anointed for the task. They play a critical role in bringing forth the prophetic message of the Lord to His people. Those who surrender their musical gift totally to the Holy Spirit are able to accurately infuse the atmosphere by stirring up the spirit of prophecy in the House like no one else. This prepares God's people for the manifestation of His will, whether it be through verbal articulation, prophetic song, or prophetic dance.

The Origin of Prophetic Song and Dance

The first prophetic song noted in the Bible occurs in Exodus 15:1-18. It is initially sung by Moses, then the

Israelites followed along. Moses was inspired by the great power that the LORD had displayed against the Egyptians by drowning them in the Red Sea while the children of Israel crossed over on dry ground. The Bible says that Moses sang this song unto the Lord right after he had witnessed the magnitude of LORD's strength and might. Why was this song considered prophetic? Because Moses, the prophet, tapped into the 'IS-ness' of God! Consider the following verses from Moses' prophetic melodies in Exodus Chapter 15:

Verse 1:   "I will sing to the LORD, for he **IS** highly exalted;"

Verse 2:   "The LORD **IS** my strength and my song, He has become my salvation; He **IS** my God and I will praise him;"

Verse 3:   "The LORD **IS** a warrior; the LORD **IS** his name!"

Verse 11:   "Who among the gods **IS** like you? Who **IS** like you—majestic in holiness; awesome in glory, working wonders?"

One may further consider the prophetic content and nature of this song due to its obvious spontaneity and relevance in the purpose of comforting, strengthening, and encouraging the Israelites through *forth telling:*

Comfort: Verse 13: "In your unfailing love you **will lead** the people whom you have redeemed; in your strength you **will guide** them";

Strengthen: Verses 14-16: "The nations **will hear and tremble**; anguish **will grip the people** of Philistia; the chiefs of Edom **will be terrified**; the leaders of Moab **will be seized** with trembling; the people of Canaan **will melt away**; terror and dread **will fall upon them.**"

Encourage: Verses 17-18: "You **will bring them in and**

plant them on the mountain of your inheritance—the place, O LORD, you made for your dwelling, the sanctuary, O LORD, your hands established. The **LORD will reign forever**."

This song of Moses' prophetic praise spawned an even more exuberant demonstration in the prophetic ministry through a celebratory, triumphant dance by his sister, Miriam the prophetess. The actions of Miriam and the women, who followed her, cite the first mention of public dance, prophetic or otherwise, in biblical history. Miriam understood then, what some are only now beginning to embrace—that just as prophecy speaks forth the word in voice and instruments, the dance minister prophesies the Word of God with his or her body. The prophetic dancer obeys the Spirit of God through an active demonstration that brings the message or experience to LIFE! These early actions of prophetic praise by Moses and Miriam would later become recognized and taught to the Israelites at the specific instruction of Moses in order to preserve, honor, and remember this transitional moment of deliverance for their descendants and for generations to come.

As the sacred artist goes forth in prophetic dance, there must be a common level of understanding, flow, and 'worship camaraderie' amongst the dancers, psalmists, musicians, and the worship leader. Most importantly for congregational ministry, the House must be one that is both accustomed and receptive to the prophetic gifts in operation. Oftentimes, the sacred dancer or dramatist may step out in movement interpretation of a prophetic message of the Lord because they are certain that they are being 'obedient to the Holy Spirit'. If the arts minister is truly operating in the flow of the Spirit, the movement/actions executed will be meaningful, appropriate, and clear to all. If this type of prophetic expression is not a regular occurrence within the culture of the congregation, it is important that a few words of explanation be said in response to this move of the Spirit immediately following. Failing to do so may allow the enemy to bring doubt and offense into the hearts and minds of the people—even to the point where some will claim that it was not of God. Before going forth in the prophetic movements of God, the sacred artist should always be mindful to confirm that they:

a. <u>Heard the **Voice** of the Holy Spirit</u>: Ask yourself—is it the Holy Spirit's unction or your own flesh prompting you to move? If you are not sure, pray and ask the Lord for confirmation that the command you heard to step out is in fact Him.

b. <u>Are in the **Timing** of the Holy Spirit</u>: Is the timing right? God loves synchronicity, but He does not like confusion. Be sure that you step out in accordance with the flow of what is happening in both the physical and the spiritual realm of the worship. God will provide just the right window of opportunity for whatever he wants to accomplish—don't miss it. Moving outside of God's timing can cause disorder, distraction, and offense. One may have indeed heard the voice of the Lord instructing them to step out into interpretation, but the timing would *not* be in the middle of the preached Word!

c. <u>Line up with the **Word** of God</u>: Do the motives, gestures, and movement interpretation line up with God's Word biblically, as well as His message that is being prophesied? For example, the prophetic word from the Lord was, "Receive My joy! Remove from your midst the spirit of heaviness; put on the garments of praise and receive your deliverance!" Yet, if the movements done come across as trite, orchestrated, and do not capture the spirit of God's message, the power of the prophetic dance will be greatly diminished.

> **Revelation:**
> One will miss their window of opportunity in bringing forth the prophetic dance if they are slow to identify the Voice of the Holy Spirit versus the voice of their own flesh.

Spontaneous or Choreographed: Can It Be Prophetic?

First and foremost, all movement executed by the sacred arts minister must be inspired by the Holy Spirit of God. In the previous example concerning Moses and Miriam, the prophetic dancing was obviously a spontaneous response to God's mighty act of deliverance and their hope for the future. However, all spontaneous movement and dance executed by the dance minister *is not prophetic*. In other words, spontaneous movement does not the prophetic dancer make!

When addressing prophetic dance movement in a worship setting, there is a clear difference between *spontaneity* and *improvisation*. When sacred dance is done **spontaneously**, it will possess the following characteristics: instinctive, unmeditated, natural, and unconstrained. On the contrary, sacred dance done **improvisationally** will possess these characteristics: inventive, concocted, contrite, and elongated.

Much of what is being observed during congregational worship and church services by their dance ministries are simply *improvised movement*. Spontaneity is a bodily reaction to what your soul and spirit feel. Improvisation is a bodily reaction to what your *eyes* observe, accompanied with what your limbs can accomplish, thus can be done with no regard to your *spiritual inclination*.

The main concern is acknowledging if in fact, the movement is inspired of the Holy Spirit. Further, if inspired by the Holy Spirit, is there a *clear message* to bring forth in movement to the Body? Or was the message an application for that individual personally? With this determined, the minister of dance must decide if the Holy Spirit has included a *'prophetic message'*, as opposed to *'a word'*, which may literally be a one word command! Remaining in this context, one may resolve that the overall nature of prophetic movement is therefore spontaneous, not improvised.

There are occasions when a sincere act of spontaneous movement will NOT be prophetic. A one-word command given in the Spirit realm, such as "Run!" may be the catalyst for the entire church to follow, thus triggering a mighty deliverance for the congregation. Yet, this command appeared to reveal no prophetic content. However, a *prophetic message* declared through movement to the congregation may bring illumination and revelation to specific individuals. Therefore, this type of message must be observed by the people and judged by the Spirit.

With this understanding of spontaneous, prophetic dance, we now address the question, "Can prophetic movement be choreographed, yet still maintain its integrity?" Absolutely yes! Choreography is the art of making creative works, usually dances, that possess specific movements, steps, patterns, and interpretations, which all come together in a meaningful, purpose-filled presentation. Now we will discover another way that God uses the sacred dance minister to declare prophetic messages to their church, society, and even their nation in order to bring about His will and purpose for His people.

<u>Prayer Declaration:</u>

Dear Lord,
Truly You are an Awesome God! Thank You for Your
Spirit, which continues to open the eyes of my heart, and
of my understanding;
Father, I yield the prophetic gifting and anointing inside
of me to Your explicit direction;
Thank you for preparing me to minister this gift to Your
Good Pleasure in humility and integrity.
Right now, I touch my ears to RECEIVE a New
HEARING in the prophetic things of God. Speak Father,
for Your servant is now in the LISTENING POSITION.
Glory to Your Name!
Amen.

Reader's Reflections:

(Fill in your own personal statements of affirmation.)

My Affirmations:

When I sense the Holy Spirit prompting me to move prophetically, I _____

_____

_____

The Word that the Spirit of God has spoken to me personally regarding my prophetic gifting is: _____

_____

_____

_____

_____

_____

_____

Sacred AFFIRMATION #12

I TAP INTO God's Hidden Wisdom for Prophetic Insight to My Destiny!

I DISCIPLINE Myself to VISUALIZE the Dance Birthed out of MY SPIRIT!

I AM RESTORED FROM Past Dreams that Tormented Me!

CHAPTER 12

Discovering the Prophetic Content of Your Dreams

"Here comes that dreamer!" they said to each other. "Come now, let's kill him and throw him into one of these cisterns and say that a ferocious animal devoured him. Then we'll see what comes of his dreams." (Genesis 37:19-20)

"For God does speak—now one way, now another—though man may not perceive it. In a dream, in a vision of the night, when deep sleep falls on men as they slumber in their beds, he may speak in their ears and terrify them with warnings, to turn man from wrongdoing and keep him from pride; to preserve his soul from the pit; his life from perishing by the sword." Job 33:14-18

Much has been written on dreams and dream interpretation from both a Christian and non-Christian perspective. It would appear, however, that many Believers today tend to shy away from publicly admitting that they do, in fact dream. In this season of unprecedented sorcery, witchcraft, psychic readings, astrology and New Age religion, it appears as though the Christian world has all but rejected one of the most powerful vehicles for receiving communication from God. Without challenge from the Body of Christ, the ungodly have been allowed to profit from these gifts that God purposed for the building up of the Kingdom. For many, the rejection of dreams as 'foolishness' is done out of fear, or at the risk of being viewed by others as weird, spooky, or super-spiritual.

However, the Bible has much to say regarding dreams. As one searches the scriptures, they will find that quite often, God communicated His will, and other significant events through the use of dreams. And that there were then and still remain today, those who can interpret them. Some theologians and ministers of the Gospel will say that God only sends dreams to those who are less able to discern the voice of God when they are coherent. Others say that dreams were primarily given to the prophets of God in order that they might maintain the integrity of the word of the LORD and fully interpret His will for the people—not their own. The implication here is that if one is truly faithful and righteous unto God, He will speak to them by His Spirit 'face to face' without the aid of dreams. Consider what God said to Miriam and Aaron in Numbers 12:6-8:

> **"When a prophet of the LORD is among you, I reveal myself to him in visions; I speak to him in dreams. But this is not true of my servant Moses; he is faithful in all my house. To him I speak face to face, clearly and not in riddles; he sees the form of the LORD."**

Regardless of the reasons and circumstances, God does

communicate with both Believers and non-Believers alike through dreams. These 'riddles' that God refers to may also be called 'parables'. Just as Jesus did His most profound teaching through the use of parables, so does the Lord often allow one to dream in *parable form*. The wonderful mystery in Jesus' motive for teaching in parables revolved around the fact that one had to crave the Truth. He used parables to veil the truth from those who were unwilling to see it. Yet, for those who really desired truth with their whole heart; they would not rest until the meaning was revealed to them. By the end of His teachings, Jesus was always able to lead his followers into the deep things of God.

A dream that may seem strange and useless to the dreamer can potentially contain a world of answers to the very prayers one has prayed! For the sacred dance minister, and countless others who are willing to embrace this fact, there is much prophetic revelation and purpose to be found in the dreams we dream. Job 33:14-18 tells us the following concerning dreams:

> **"For God does speak—now one way, now another—though man may not perceive it. In a dream, in a vision of the night, when deep sleep falls on men as they slumber in their beds, he may speak in their ears and terrify them with warnings, to turn man from wrongdoing and keep him from pride; to preserve his soul from the pit; his life from perishing by the sword."**

God's dreams may serve as 'supernatural wisdom' with the capability to accomplish the following:

> To **warn and terrify from sin;** to **guide through repentance**; to **preserve one's soul and life**.

Dreams that Warn and Terrify

First, in order to believe that God is able to 'warn and ter-rify' us from sin, we should know that God definitely has His way of communicating with Believers and non-Believers, the godly and the ungodly. In the years prior to my salvation, I am now 100% sure that many of the dreams I had were God's way of getting my attention in a personally mysterious, and usually, very fearful way. I realized after the fact that this was *not* the devil's doing. God may warn us of impending danger or consequences for our wrongful actions and choices through dreams. And, if one's choice is to ignore Him, He may also terrify an individual so much that it actually scares one out of the very temptation to commit sin.

Consider how the Lord terrified King Abimelech in a dream in Genesis 20:3 saying, "You are as good as dead because the woman you have taken is a married woman." This woman was Sarah, wife of Abraham—two biblical stalwarts of faith. Although Abimelech was wrongly told that Sarah was Abraham's sister, the Lord still chose to ter-rify him from contemplating this act of adultery. The Gospel of Matthew clearly cites the Lord giving divine instructions of warning through dreams to Joseph in Matthew 1:20. The Lord warns Joseph not to 'put away' his espoused wife Mary because surely, her conception was done of the Holy Spirit—not of man. Joseph received this as truth, keeping Mary's honor as his wife. In another instance during the time of Christ's birth, the kings who came from afar to wor-ship the baby Jesus in Bethlehem were also warned by God in a dream not to report Christ's whereabouts to King Herod, less the baby be killed. (Matthew 1:8-12)

Later we see in Matthew 1:13 how the Lord sent Joseph yet another urgent message through a dream warning him to take up his family and flee to Egypt before Herod could find Jesus and destroy him. Here, the family would live safely among the Egyptians until the time of Herod's death.

If the sacred artist was to minister from a prophetic dream received whose overall message/theme was that of 'warning', the presentation would probably be a form of warfare. The purpose is to warn *away* from sin, which means the Holy Spirit aims to convict and convince strongly. The movements and thematic gestures will undoubtedly be aggressive, direct, urgent and compelling; almost desperate in nature. If music is used, it must match the intensity of the prophetic message delivered. One may also choose to deliver this message either through a choreo-drama, or other dramatic presentation.

Dreams to Bring Repentance

Sometimes, God desires to bring individuals to repentance from sin through divine revelation in dreams, as was the case with King Nebuchadnezzar in Daniel 4:18-27. Unfortunately, like many Believers and non-Believers alike, the king chose not to renounce his sins and wickedness, therefore the consequential fulfillment of his ignorance began just one year later. One of the least discussed circumstances of God's desire for repentance through a dream is in the case of the wife of Pontius Pilate in Matthew 27:19. This woman received a revelatory dream which was described by her as "painful and troubling, causing intense suffering". This dream caused her to send word to her husband while he sat at the judgement seat. She told him that not only was Jesus an innocent man, but that Pilate should "turn and have nothing to do with him".

Prophetic movement purposed to draw individuals to repentance can be very powerful. Usually, this type of ministry will cause individuals in need of repentance to have a supernatural revelation of the holiness of God. Prophetic dreams ministered on repentance will carry a heavy anointing of conviction towards sin. It is the type of anointing which does not condemn, rather it compels one to see the filthiness of their sin, alongside the righteousness of God. This usually forces one to respond as Isaiah said, "Woe is me, I am ruined—for I am a man of unclean lips"! (Isa. 6:5)

Dreams for the Preservation of One's Life and Soul

The preservation of one's life and soul speaks of the overall well being of an individual. In Genesis Chapter 41:14 through Chapter 45:11, God revealed prophetic plans and purposes through Pharaoh and Joseph. When Pharaoh received a mysterious dream that none of his other servants could interpret, he called for Joseph—then a slave, whose gift Pharaoh had heard about. Through divine interpretation, Joseph alerted Pharaoh of his kingdom's inevitable destiny— seven years of plenty and seven years of famine. Through the wisdom of God, Joseph assisted in saving the lives of thousands who may have otherwise died during the famine. Joseph advised Pharaoh that each city must build up great storehouses of food and goods during the season of plenty.

In the process of time, God allowed Pharaoh's dream to intersect with Joseph's dream as a young boy (Genesis 37:5-9)—that is that his own brother's would one day worship him and that he would be in leadership over them. Prophetic fulfillment of the dreams were triggered when during the time of famine, the Lord caused Joseph's brothers to come to him, now in rulership, seeking food and provisions for their household. God used a dream from years ago to bring about reconciliation and restoration in the lives and souls of Joseph's brothers. Joseph's compassion and this restoration proved to preserve them from the consequences of their sin towards Joseph. We must never grow weary of seeing the fulfillment of our God-inspired dreams! Though it may tarry, wait on it because it will surely come! These dreams, when ministered prophetically, are full of mercy, rejoicing, and celebration.

Each of these accomplishments—warning, terrifying,

repentance, and preservation of life, has prophetic implications. It is this understanding that qualifies the sacred dance minister to make the connection between prophecy and dreams. Recalling now the **three key uses** for prophecy, along with the **three accomplishments made** through the use of dreams, one may correlate the two gifts as so:

3 KEY USES FOR PROPHECY: (1Corinthians 14:1-3)	3 ACCOMPLISHMENTS OF DREAMS: (Job 33:14-18)
1. Comfort	Preserves One's Soul and One's Life
2. Strengthening	Warns and Terrifies Us from Sin
3. Encouragement	Turns Us to Repentance and Humility

Where Is Your Journal?

Whether in parables, scenes, symbols, 'word pictures' or the emotions one feels during and after, God desires to reveal His prophetic wisdom through dreams. Unfortunately, they are usually dismissed as mere coincidence or 'something I ate last night'. For individuals who are not in the habit of voice recording, keeping a journal, or discussing significant dreams with trusted friends, more than likely, the dream will be forgotten from their memories. Imagine losing a very important letter. Now imagine that the letter is from God! The Lord does not send us undeliverable or 'junk' mail—anything He sends is of vital importance to us! The prophet Isaiah speaks in Chapter 55:10-11 saying:

> **"As the heavens are higher than the earth, so are my ways higher than your ways and my**

thoughts than your thoughts. As the rain and the snow come down from heaven, and do not return to it without watering the earth and making it bud and flourish, so that it yields seed for the sower and bread for the eater, so is my word that goes out from my mouth: It will not return to me empty, but will ACCOM-PLISH what I desire and achieve the purpose for which I sent it.'

The discipline of maintaining regular documentation of our dreams, special moments, or revelations from God to us specifically cannot be understated. As you continue this practice, God will begin to fulfill personal prayers and promises that will have eternal implications to your destiny in the earth. Get a journal and begin to use it **now.** With every word you write, imagine that you are loosening every shackle that has bound you, sealing satan's defeat, and soaring your way along the path of your success!

Too many of us, especially within the Diaspora, have allowed uniquely divine revelation given to us from the throne of God, to go unpenned, unpublished, and unprophesied. We have run after what the masses deem as a 'Rhema Word', which oftentimes ends up being a re-worked concept of a 10-year-old message. God has ordained and positioned some of you to be deliverers of a confused, hurting, nation of people. He has revealed answers and plans of action to you that have seemingly baffled others for centuries. Yet, because of a lack of discipline, procrastination, and unbelief, you have delayed bringing forth the dreams God has given you. In fact, sacred artist—by now, you should have written your own book, daily devotional, commentary, song, production, play or movie, which has the exact anointing needed to set captives free and deliver nations! Don't allow your human infirmities to cause you to miss your window of opportunity. Come now, take the Lord's dreams and make them yours—Pen it! Publish it! Prophesy it!

The Holy Spirit inspires one to **PROPHESY**—to foretell, bring forth, and CONFESS those things that be not, as though they ARE; the **DREAM** is the preparation for what is yet to come. The **DANCE** is the prophetic MANIFESTATION of a dream that resides in the heart and mind of the Father!

The goal of the prophetic dance minister should be to execute with precision, the delivery of prophetic movement interpretation inspired of the Holy Spirit through dreams, visions, and verbal instruction from the Spirit of God.

Daydreaming...and I'm Thinking of You

Do not misunderstand—dreams do not only occur at night when one is sleeping. These are not the kind of daydreams one may have while the preacher delivers his or her message, and one thinks of what they may have for dinner later. Nor are these the kind of daydreams that cause individuals to fantasize about special 'encounters' with the opposite sex. Many individuals daydream, see visions, and have what may be described as *'encounters with God'* on a regular basis. Paul was not asleep when he spoke of his many revelations and visions that he had in 2Corinthians Chapter 12, saying that he was "caught up to the third heaven—whether in the body, or out of the body, I do not know—God knows." John was not asleep when by the Spirit, he received the apocalyptic prophecy recorded in the book of Revelation Chapter 1:10 saying, "On the Lord's Day, I was in the Spirit, and I heard behind me a loud voice like a trumpet which said: 'Write on a scroll what you see and send it to the seven churches...' ".

The prophetic dance minister will sometimes, 'dream' during the Worship Service Experience. For some, a powerful unction of the Spirit or a song carrying an unusually strong anointing will cause the dance minister to visualize movement in scenes, word-pictures, or concepts—this later develops into *choreography*. He or she may begin to move or dance in an attitude of prophetic interpretation as a result of what the Holy Spirit is *speaking* into their hearts and *showing* them in their mind's eye. It is then that the discerning congregation of worshippers either follows the individual's lead, or simply observes and sees the Word of the Lord manifested in movement. The dance minister's posture and position will dictate whether the Holy Spirit is calling for congregational dance or if the Lord has a particular word to convey through His vessel.

Just as with any prophecy, a dream received from the Lord must be contextualized. In other words, it must be viewed in line with the Word of God, as well as in the context of the dreamer's life, situation, and circumstances. Every word of prophecy revealed is not always meant for everyone to hear, nor is every dream the Lord gives an individual meant to be shared with others. In the Body of Christ, there is still much work to be done in the areas of true brotherhood, sisterhood, and general Christian camaraderie—the kind that compels us to cheer for one another's successes, accomplishments, hopes, and fulfillment of a dream. A mean, arrogant, and competitive spirit hovers within the ranks of many anointed ministers and artists. Until they fall, these individuals will only be concerned with promoting themselves. Thank God for those kingdom-minded servants and handmaidens who are able to catch the viable dreams of another and run alongside the visionary to see it come to fruition. However, until we all come into that knowledge…

Dream Your Dance, Dance Your Dream

One anointed musician and Gospel artist who has testified about the power of dreams in his own artistic expression is Minister Richard Smallwood. In his song entitled, "Healing", he states:

"The Lord gave me this song in a dream...and when I woke up, I knew that this was the healing song..."

Many sacred arts ministers dream about their particular art form. This is especially true of the sacred dance minister. Personally speaking, it is quite common for the Holy Spirit to choreograph entire dance interpretations, or choreo-dramas through a dream; most often, these dreams will be prophetic in content. The Lord may also decide to place a certain passage of scripture in one's spirit in an attempt to speak very literally or directly to the individual.

Revelation:
The goal of the prophetic dance minister is to execute with precision, the delivery of pure, prophetic movement interpretation inspired of the Holy Spirit through dreams, visions, and verbal instruction from the Spirit of God.

How does one go about interpreting and disciphering the dreams that reside in the heart of God? The answer to this question must be preceded with some preliminary guidelines. In general, one should not try to force unfounded meaning to a dream by making quick judgements and conclusions about what the Lord may be saying. For example, a dream about death, whether our own or a loved one's, should not always be viewed literally and as something to be alarmed about. It may be that this 'death' is symbolic of repentance and humility (1Corinthians 15:31), or a spiritual death that allows God's gifts to be multiplied. (John 12:24) In another instance, an individual may have frequent dreams and visions of the past—either a situation or a person they may have known. This may be God's way of alerting the person that it is time for them to address, or resolve past hurts and issues—God's desire here may be to bring healing to a particular area of one's life. (Matthew 4:7-39)

While there are many interpretations that any individual could place upon an isolated dream, the sacred dance minister seeks out the ONE that is MOST ACCURATE AND RELEVANT to what the Spirit is saying during that particular season. The dance minister seeking to manifest the prophetic content of their dreams through movement will discover that some basic characteristic comparisons between dreams and prophetic dance will assist them in bringing forth the message from the Lord most effectively. Whether in spontaneous movement, or set choreography inspired by a prophetic dream, the sacred dance minister will find the following similarities to be present:

1. Dreams and prophetic dance alike almost always require interpretation.

2. Just as dreams usually contain more than one 'scene', prophetic movement interpretation usually contains a series of movements as opposed to one basic gesture.

3. Both dreams and prophetic movement contain a progressive message or theme that unfolds before the eyes of the viewer(s).

4. During both dreams and prophetic movement, the individual is either:
   a. An active participant who testifies to the encounter personally OR
   b An observer who is carried along through each 'scene' or phase of the encounter

As one allows the Holy Spirit to develop their desire to hear, recognize, and know the voice of God in any way He chooses to make Himself known, one will naturally become more keenly aware of those dreams and visions that are <u>not</u> from the Father. Contrary to some beliefs, the fact that a dream/vision may have been 'scary' or unsettling, disturbing, and the like, does not automatically indicate that the dream is from the enemy—God may be trying to get the person's attention!

First and foremost, the sacred dance minister understands the absolute necessity of being 'covered' in prayer, because everything one *thinks* they hear is not from God. Understanding this, it is important that as one receives a dream or vision into their spirit, they should retain only that which is in accordance to the Word of God. If it is truly from God, it will be consistent with His word, no matter the nature of it. 2Timothy 3:16-17 says,

"All Scripture is God-breathed and is useful for teaching, rebuking, correcting, and training in righteousness, so that the man of God may be thoroughly equipped for every good work."

Dreams or visions that contain overtones of witchcraft, cultism, unusually violent episodes, killing, chaos, and confusion are not of God. Do not be deceived into thinking that the Lord is using these kinds of dreams to call you into spiritual warfare—not so, for we already understand that we **are presently** in a war. These types of dreams are direct assaults from the devil and must not be tolerated nor entertained. It is possible that the dreamer is experiencing some inner turmoil that the enemy has detected, therefore he has sent out his demons to trouble the person's spirit. Sometimes, individuals may have exposed themselves unknowingly to subtle satanic practices, or may have left a door open through some unresolved area of sin in their lives. However, one will also find that if the enemy is harshly tormenting them in their dreams, God will intervene through the insertion of a sudden thought or a way of escape during the encounter.

With this said, now the interpretation can begin! The following steps serve only as a guide to assist the sacred dance minister to begin to pull out the prophetic content of his or her dreams so that they may be danced in the fullness, in the glory, and in the purposes of God. They are referred to as, *"Pathways to Dreaming the Dance and Dancing the Dream"*. This approach to dance ministry is sure to revolutionize the way one would typically approach choreography and interpretive movement. Just as prophets and preachers alike crave a fresh word from the Lord, the dance minister longs for a fresh, relevant, and innovative message that comes straight from the heart of God. Giving oneself over completely to the Holy Spirit for the use of the prophetic ministry will allow the dance minister to be free from the expectations of others. Diligent meditation on the Word of God, submission to the Holy Spirit of God, and an intense hope for the future fulfillment of every word spoken through the Holy Scriptures will propel the prophetic dancer into new realms of delightfulness in GOD. It will arm them with a newfound freedom to dream what others continue to call the *impossible dream.*

Pathways to Dreaming the Dance and Dancing the Dream

1. **Intercession:** The act of intercession places you in the proper position to receive the will of God. If you are not an intercessor, the Lord may rarely attempt to communicate with you through dreams; you will be less likely to readily gain an understanding of the dream, and He knows that part of your natural instinct will be to dismiss it. Therefore, every sacred artist should have a strong prayer life, and an even stronger propensity for

intercession. Praying in the Spirit is key in 'preparing the ground', that is, the mind, to receive the word of the Lord. Romans 8:27 says, "He who searches our hearts knows the mind of the Spirit because the Spirit intercedes for the saints in accordance with God's will."

2. **Write It Down:** Instead of rushing out of bed immediately in the morning, take time to wake up properly. Upon waking, greet your Father with a pleasant "Good Morning, Lord!". Next, ask the Holy Spirit to bring any dreams you may have had back to your remembrance with clarity. Your 'dream journal' should be nearby— record the date, time, and your current location. This information is important because the message that the Lord is speaks to you may have specific relevance to the country you are in or the people who are around you. For example, your entry may say: "January 1, 2002; 6:00am—Johannesburg, South Africa". As you write, try to record as much of the significant details as you can. Write it just the way you dreamed it.

3. **Identify Key Words and Symbols:** With the dream recorded in its entirety, go back and highlight certain key words, phrases, and symbols found within the body of your dream. This is a very important step. One must be able to discern the things that are significant to the overall interpretation of the message, while ignoring those things that are vague and have no added value. The key words may be categorized very basically as people, places, things, colors, numbers, words, actions, animals, and scripture.

4. **Use Your Bible Resources:** There are 4 fundamental resources that the Believer may use when interpreting a message from the Spirit of God. Among them are the

Bible, a Complete or an Exhaustive Concordance, a good Bible Dictionary, and a reputable Bible Commentary. These powerful tools will assist you in keeping your dream in its proper context, as well as getting an understanding about what the Bible says regarding the key words and symbolism.

5. **Allow the Holy Spirit to Give You Further Insight:** At this point, your dream journal or notebook pages will be filled with words, phrases, scripture references, and other special notes you may jot down with reference to what you are discovering. The pages may appear to be like 'word puzzles'—meaningless and disorderly. Take this opportunity to close your journal and go into a season of prayer and meditation. Silence seems to work well during this time, as the Holy Spirit will begin to bring light and revelation to the true message that God wants delivered. It is also in this season when the Holy Spirit may begin to show the sacred dancer a movement vocabulary to accompany some of the key action words that were previously highlighted. Resist the temptation to begin to dance out what you see—this is only the beginning of the revelation; simply be still, hear, and SEE what the Spirit is revealing.

6. **Begin to REPLACE the Symbols with Their Meaning:** Return to your journal. For each symbol recorded, you probably have a few words, phrases, and maybe even scripture which supports the biblical meaning of the symbol highlighted from your dream as potentially significant. This step is an exciting one as it truly begins to put the pieces of the puzzle together. For example, if in a recorded dream, I documented that I saw many mountains, I may have high-

lighted **'mountain'** as one of my key symbols. In Step #4, as I utilized my Bible Resources, I noted the following about **'mountains'**:

<u>My notes on MOUNTAINS:</u> *characteristics*—a high place, a large, great mass; also referred to as a 'mount'. Many famous mountains are mentioned throughout the Scriptures as a result of some **significant and miraculous happenings**. Among them were: Mount Sinai (the mountain of God or of the Law); Mount Nebo (the place of Moses' death); Mount Zion (the mountain upon which Jerusalem was built) and Mount Hermon (believed to be the scene of the Transfiguration).

Mountains were used in scripture as a strong place of **refuge and shelter** (Gen. 14:19; Ps. 11:1; 1Sam. 23:14); as a place of **worship and holiness** (Ps. 87:1; Is. 56:7, 57:13; Dan. 11:45; Joel 3:17; John 4:20); and symbolic of the **nations** (Rev. 17:9, 15). Mountains also represented a great **challenge or obstacle** (Matt. 17:20).

Now equipped with a fuller understanding of the depth of that one word, I may summarize by saying:

Mountains = A significant or miraculous thing to come; God's protection; a new level of worship; challenges are on the way, but not impossible; called to the nations.

This exercise may be done with each of the highlighted words, phrases, symbols, until the individual feels confident in the clarity of the prophetic message that God is speaking. The above example was just <u>one symbol</u>—imagine what the message may say in its entirety! While each symbol may not lend itself to great detail, others will. Usually the Holy Spirit is able to reveal the meaning of the message with the aid of just a few words. After all of the symbols have been replaced with their proper meanings, the end result may be a prophetic declaration that may be spoken, preached, sung, or danced into manifestation! The **prophetic declaration** for the **'mountain'** example may sound something like this:

> *"The Lord is calling you to transform the Nations with your gift. He desires to reveal Himself through you in great and miraculous ways. These ways will cause you to lead His people to new heights of worship and accountability to holiness that has yet to be seen. Because you have exalted His name high above the mountains, He will cause you to walk along high places in the earth. There will be challenges along the way that will cause you to doubt His calling upon your life, but know this—God's strong Hand of protection is with you and nothing is impossible with Him."*

A dream in and of itself has no value unless the dreamer takes hold of it and squeezes out every ounce of prophetic potential contained inside. The dreams of God will lay dormant in one's mind and journal unless they seize the urgency of the moment. Procrastination is not an option. It is in this moment, in this season, that the sacred artist and the Believer, who understand the power of a dream will speak to their legs, saying, "PRAY!" and suddenly, the dance begins.

The dance you dream is born out of your very own spirit, therefore, there will be none like it in the entire universe! No one will be able to reproduce it! But YOU, the dreamer, by the power of the Holy Spirit, can bring forth a supernatural impartation into the lives of all who are willing to receive it. **Time** is of the essence. There are millions of hopeless children and adults who don't know that they are allowed to dream—let alone that they can DANCE their dreams! It is the responsibility of those who **know** and can testify to the fact that nothing is impossible when the hand of the Lord is with you. We must teach others how to make effective use of their dreams—that is, how to envision their dreams as a healing path ordained by God. Our children must know that they have the right to dream—that they carry within them God-given treasures and hidden mysteries that will lead us into the future. They must know that their gift is **not magic.**

Children armed with this knowledge and freedom allow God's healing power to flow in the lives of those who have been wounded at the hands of others. This knowledge will also allow God's joy to flow in those same little lives whose faces, once aglow with innocence and hope, now stare back at us in despair and fear.

Beach Dance

During a Saturday session of creative dance class, one of my 4 year-olds stood in the middle of the floor while everyone else continued to follow me in movement. All at once the little girl flopped down on the floor and began to cry. After a barrage of questions about what could possibly be upsetting her, she tearfully and calmly said, "Auntie Stephanie, I want to go to the beach". I was absolutely amused and intrigued. This child was daydreaming—in *my* class. She had gotten a revelation and became so passionate, to the point of tears. Soon the 'beach anointing' came over the other children in the class. As they caught the vision, they literally began to run with it! I quickly directed the children to gather in the center of the floor. I asked the same little girl to describe what she *saw* when she thought of the beach. The other children chimed in. Children whom *I knew* couldn't even swim began to envision themselves swimming out into the deep blue sea! These children assisted me in catching the vision! We began the Beach Dance, equipped with dancers serving as the sand, the sea, the sun, the breeze, and the trees—anything that moved! A wonderful spirit of happiness took over the class. As I saw the children (and even myself) being set free from their fears of the ocean and inhibitions about their bodies, it inspired me to set a prophetic, choreographic piece for the children to the song by Ron Kenoly entitled, "Happiness, Peace, Joy in the Holy Ghost". The dance encouraged boldness, positive self-identity, and Kingdom authority. This is just one example of how godly indulgence in a child's 'daydream' can bring forth emotional healing, spiritual impartation and blessings poured out upon the entire class—This is what is meant by birthing a dance 'out of your own spirit'!

A Final Word from the Father

The Dance of LIFE in its entirety is all-inclusive. The joy, the pain, the sunshine, and the RAIN!

Could it be that *you* are carrying within your Body-Temple that 'secret thing' which will activate the manifestation of the Coming of our Lord Jesus Christ as prophesied in Revelation 22:12?

> **"Behold, I am coming soon! My reward is with me, and I will give it to everyone according to what he has done. I am the Alpha and the Omega, the First and the Last, the Beginning and the End."**

The reward to be given to us from the King will be contingent upon what we have *done*. All of us are called to **action**. Sacred artists, you must realize that your nation, and the nations of the world are waiting to receive *your gift*, which brings the Good News of the Gospel that saves, delivers, heals, judges and reconciles the people of the world from generation to generation. You must dare to unleash the fury, the fire, and the passion of the Living God through the discipline that He has assigned to you from birth. Your season for searching, pondering, procrastinating, laying hold of, and praying about revelation of your true calling and position is *over*. If you are chosen and called into the priesthood of the Sacred Artist, the Father says to you:

"Behold My Sons and My Daughters,
On this day, I shall make it plain.
You are My Bridge to the Nations and you will serve
*   as a strong source—as a beam for many.*
As I move you, you will bring entire nations together
*   for the purpose of reconciliation*
through My Sacred Arts;
Many will cross over you, my great bridge;
I will make your body to be strong and whole; I will
*   make your body to be as an octopus with many*
*   tentacles;*
These will be your Arms, able to reach My people in
*   many directions and stages of life;*
As My Bridge to the Nations, you will lead others as I
*   have led you;*
You will stir up the gifts inside of them and propel
*   them into My Way of thinking—My Kingdom*
*   mindset;*
Yes, their ways will be radically transformed and as
*   you stretch yourself, I will strengthen you;*
You will reach back and you, yourself will strengthen
*   your brothers and sisters with a pure love—*
This is what will help them to cross over;
You are My Bridge to the Nations;
Then, after a Time, you will look up and see the work
*   of your hands;*
You will look back at the path you have walked and
*   see those demons that together, we have slayed!*
You will look around and see thousands upon thou-
*   sands of people to whom you have birthed into*
*   My Ministry;*

And at that time, you will hear the heart of your
Father saying, "This is my beloved in whom I'm
exceedingly pleased."
Only keep your body holy unto Me and bring honor,
not shame, to My Name;
Dance the dance for which I formed you;
That is, the Nation Dance; the dance that never
ceases to draw My people to Me from the ends of
the earth."
As you go, be strong and very courageous; when you
hesitate, know that I am with you indeed;
My ever-present favor is a force field around you and
not one hair from your head shall be harmed;
You are My Bridge to the Nations."

This prophetic declaration from the Lord has two powerful revelations to the minister of the Arts. First, God has
referred to us as His 'bridge to the Nations'. This says that
God has extremely high expectations of how we must fulfil
our destinies. He compares us in the spirit realm to a
bridge—intricate, strong, reliable, skillfully crafted, and
resourceful in ability to transport oneself and others from
one level to another. He says that just as the base of a bridge
is deeply rooted in the waters, (symbolic of the Holy Spirit),
so will we be. Furthermore, bridges accomplish a life-long
necessity—that is, the bridge assists in carrying individuals
over what might otherwise be called 'dangerous waters'.

The significance of the Lord referring to us as His Bridge
to the Nations brings into focus His unswerving concern for
all nations of the world. He reminds the true sacred arts ministers that it is not His will for our ministries to be stagnant
and isolated in one specific place. You may begin in one location, but a bridge *reaches*, stretches, and broadens itself geo-
graphically. The nations are our pulpits—not the four walls of
our church or the geographical boundaries of our cities.

The second portion of the revelation comes towards the end of the Father's message to us. He says that we must "dance the dance for which I formed you—that is the Nation Dance". Each of God's anointed artists hold within them a **key**. Biblically and spiritually, a 'key' is symbolic of wisdom and authority. Just prior to our Lord Jesus' Ascension, He told his disciples that He would give them the "keys to the Kingdom" and that the gates of Hell would not prevail against it. God's desire has always been that we would endeavor to understand the inter-workings and systems of His Kingdom. The truth is that we have had the keys in our hands since the day we became baptized and empowered by the Holy Spirit of God. However, the keys were being used incorrectly; attempting to unlock the wrong doors.

Each of our God-ordained territorial assignments in ministry require a different key to unlock the dance of a nation. We cannot use the same key, or the same wisdom exercised in one nation, to bring forth the *sacred dance* of another nation. Indeed, God has granted each nation its own Dance. It is a wonderful mystery that comes to us in parable form. In the assignment of the sacred artist, he or she must be willing to completely open their consecrated Body-Temple to the spirit of the nation assigned to them. This can be dangerous, as one may in fact find themselves in a nation of spiritual wickedness and iniquity. Your vessel must be **completely** yielded to the Lord, less you fall into temptation and adapt the practices of 'Babylon'.

However, for the yielded vessel, the spirit of holiness will reside and rest upon you. This sacred artist discovers that in the complete giving of themselves to a nation, they are able to tap into the nation's unique pulse—that is their blood line as well as their rhythm. The Nation Dance comes forth through one's Godly compassion and yearning to understand life questions: What makes the nation cry? What excites and brings joy to the nation? What concerns the nation? What infuriates the nation? What is keeping hope alive in the nation? One cannot find the answers to these questions through simple observation, nor can they be found solely through the pages of history books. Never trust yourself to make assumptions and draw conclusions based on the 'apparent' state of things in the natural. While these methods will bring about some truth, the real answers will only be revealed by the Spirit. The more open and yielded the Body-Temple, the broader and deeper the revelation will become. Sometimes these answers cannot be spoken, nor should they be.

The answers to these questions, and others like it are the things a Nation must sing about. These are the things a Nation must Dance about! Wisdom will dictate how the glorious priesthood of sacred artists will covertly, yet deliberately overtake all that has been grossly perverted at the hands of the enemy, *and* carnal Christians. This is not a new thing, as many early trailblazers in the Arts have laid the groundwork for the violent days that we now find ourselves in.

The assignment of each 21st Century minister of the Arts is to radically, progressively come forth in ways that positively infiltrate and challenge the minds of our youth and our communities.

Understanding that we have been transformed into God's Bridge to the Nations makes us accountable to standing in the gap—interceding THROUGH holy artistry, between the past, the present, and the future generation of warring, worshipping, and conquering Artists until the Day that Jesus returns!

Hebraic Movement Word Study and Commentary

This segment will focus on 6 Hebrew words of praise, that when activated in a sincere, open vessel (you) will usher in the presence of the Lord. Each of the Hebrew terms may be found in the *Strong's Exhaustive Concordance.*

1. <u>**TOWDAH:**</u> A frank, open, and intentional declaration with the extension of the hands. It may be used as a sign of surrender, or a thanksgiving offering to the Lord.

"I will enter His gates with thanksgiving and come into His courts with praise..." (Psalm 100:4)

Entering the House of the Lord, or entering His presence with uplifted hands will compel your mind and the rest of your body to be open and ready for all that God has in store for you. A true and sincere Towdah is done in the spirit of humility of heart. It will force one to 'prostrate their hearts' before the Lord simultaneously as they lift up their hands to Him. Thanksgiving is offered, confessions are made, and God prepares one's own 'Body-Temple' for an intimate encounter with the Holy Spirit. This expression of Towdah is the first level of praise leading into the worship experience. Other scriptural references for the expression of 'Towdah' include: **Leviticus 22:29; 2Chronicles 5:13; Ezra 10:11; Psalm 42:4; Psalm 134:2; 1Timothy 2:8.**

2. **YADAH:** Hand power; a waving of the hands; hands that give power and direction; to throw away or to throw at; to revere in worship. 'Yadah' is an expression used to confess, to praise, or to give thanks in the hands with the focus Jehovah God. In Isaiah 14:27, the prophet says, "For what the Lord has purposed, who can thwart Him? His *hand* is stretched out, who can turn it back?" This scripture, and many others like it symbolize the power of an outstretched hand. It is vital for the Believer to readily embrace the many aspects of the physicality of the Father. While God is indeed Spirit, He relates to His children in a way that allows one to experience the spiritual reality of His humanity and this is a wonderful thing!

In Exodus 29:20, the Lord instructs:

"Take the other ram, and Aaron and his sons shall lay their hands on its head. Slaughter it, take some of its blood and put it on the lobes of the right ears of Aaron and his sons, on the thumbs of their right hands, and on the big toes of their right feet."

Aaron and his sons the priests had to first lay hands on the beast in order to sanctify and purify it before the sacrifice. The blood from this same beast was applied to their right ears, indicating a cleansing, as well as a need clearly hear and listen to the voice of Jehovah God. The blood applied to the thumbs of the right hands was symbolic of the dominant strength and ability found in the hands. The blood applied to the right toes represented God's command for His chosen servants to walk uprightly in holiness, discernment, and godliness. In essence, God's special anointing and consecration of these individuals in such a peculiar way established a principle of HEARING (ear) right, so that one may be compelled to DO (hand) right, in order that they might WALK/LIVE (toe) right.

The priests and Levites dedicated 'wave offerings' unto the Lord. That is, their animal sacrifices as an offering of thanksgiving and atonement. Today, we wave our own hands to declare our praise, but also in order to declare the power and authority God has given us over the enemy. There is priestly power right in the palm of our hands! This 'yadah' or 'hand power' has the ability to supernaturally declare war in the heavenlies with one simple wave! It has the ability to make satan flee with directive authority. These hands, when directed in movement and dance, also have the power to prophesy!

In Ezekiel 21:14, the Lord commands, "You therefore, Son of Man, strike your hands together and prophesy; the third time, let the sword do double damage". The same power that God imposed upon the prophet Ezekiel is ours as we acknowledge that our God is a God of ACTION and MOVEMENT! He continues to demonstrate the greatness and strength that He has placed within our Body-Temples so that we will function as His weapons of honor against the kingdom of darkness. When we extend ourselves to God in an act of 'yadah', we literally stretch our spirits towards the Father's Spirit so that upon impact, the supernatural occurs. Other scriptural references for the expression of 'Yadah' include: **Genesis 29:35; Leviticus 16:21; Leviticus 26:40; Isaiah 25:1; 2Chronicles 31:2**

3. **CHAGAG:** To celebrate together; to move in a circle; to reel to and fro. 'Chagag' indicates an exuberant and lavish form of demonstrative celebration and enjoyment. Several biblical references to this expression are accompanied with

the act of participating in traditional Festivals. Still other references to this expression of celebration are accompanied with laughter. Celebration may be used interchangeably with the act of dancing. This is particularly significant throughout the Bible and within the Jewish culture as the celebration of festivals is used to commemorate the mighty saving acts of God. The LORD referred to them as, 'My Feasts' because they are the Sacred Memorial Banquets to which all of His people were invited. There were at least seven different feasts or festivals that were recognized and kept sacred unto the Lord. Leviticus 23:1-4 says, "And the LORD spoke unto Moses, saying, "Speak unto the children of Israel, and say unto them, concerning the Feasts of the LORD, which you shall proclaim to be Holy Convocations, even these are MY FEASTS! ... These are the Feasts of the LORD, even Holy Convocations, which you shall proclaim in their seasons." The LORD's festivals were initially given to the people of Israel, for it was His plan that through them salvation was to be proclaimed to the world. A Holy Convocation is a commanded assembly. It is a time when one is required to join together with fellow worshippers of the Almighty God. One may compare the movements that took place during these celebrations to what naturally occurs today within the Diasporic Christian community, known as 'congregational worship dancing'. Individuals of African, Caribbean, Hispanic, Indian, and Eastern European heritage are intrinsically a 'dancing people'. Therefore, celebration and joyous demonstration follows them within the life of their worship and beyond. Today, many Protestant churches have begun to adapt and embrace corporate worship in this manner. In any event, the feasts themselves, as well as any expression of 'chagag', in done as a spiritual offering and memorial to the LORD alone. Other scriptural references for expressions of 'Chagag' include: **Exodus 12:14; Exodus 23:14-16; Psalm 42:4-5; Zechariah 14:16; Psalm 107:27.**

4. **RAQAD:**To stomp; to spring about wildly; to jump, leap, and skip. The expression of 'raqad' is seen frequently during a Spirit-Filled worship experience. One may find a worshipper who may begin to 'stamp' their feet when the Spirit moves upon them. Sometimes, this stamping evolves into a march or a 'treading' which may be a sign of personal breakthrough in deliverance or spiritual warfare. To the onlooker, this particular expression can sometimes appear to be extreme and out of control. However, when one is under the influence of the Holy Spirit, all is well. For instance, in many of our worship experiences, it is not uncommon to see men and women at various points begin in expressions of 'Raqad', stomping, jumping, and springing about. When this occurs, many well-meaning ushers and attendants will immediately begin to encircle the individual, lock hands, and move around the individual—as if the person has been placed in confinement! The assumption here is that the person may injure themselves, or another person near to them. On the contrary, when the Holy Spirit manifests through intense stomping, jumping, or treading, there should be no interference or stifling of the deliverance process. In Nahum 3:2, the expression of 'raqad' is comparable to that of galloping horses at war. There are also scripture texts that make references to nature, animals, and persons who express their action of 'raqad' through strong skipping, dancing about, and repeated stamping of the feet. Other scriptural references for the expression of 'raqad' include: **1Chronicles 15:29, Job 21:11, Ps.29:6, Psalm 114:4, and Psalm 29:6**

Revelation:
I have always had the power to break free inside of me. Satan knew it—Now that I <u>believe</u> it, the devil is panicking.

---

5. **KARAR:**To spin and to whirl about. The expression of 'karar' is one of the most powerful expressions for the sacred dance minister to engage in. When executed with precision and clarity, the witnesses to this expression in movement may simply view the individual as a well-trained technician. However, in the spiritual realm, the dance minister may place the 'karar' in two categorical uses: deliverance and joy. As one spins and whirls about with holy abandon, spiritual bondages and chains are loosed. It is as if the individual strategically spins his or her way out of the hands of the enemy and into the joy of the Lord. The spiritual rope unravels and when the Holy Spirit signals, the spirit of liberation takes place in the soul of the dancer. This is the freedom required in order for the dance minister to flow freely according to the will of the Father. The act of spinning and whirling about takes us back to our childhood, recalling times of simplicity, innocence, and naivete. Matthew 18:3 tells us that it is the Father's will that we would come to Him as little children. The expression of 'karar' is a special gift and weapon from God given to us, His children. One may begin their spin in innocence, yet may end it in spiritual warfare, desperately seeking deliverance from a physical, emotional, or psychological prison. It is in this moment that the window of opportunity exists for the dancer to be made whole. Even as one spins and tears begin to fall, the enemy loses his grip on our lives. Soon, we proclaim as the Psalmist did in Psalm 30:11, that God has indeed "turned our wailing into dancing and has removed our sackcloth and clothed us with joy"! This is what caused King David to dance out of his garments. According to 2Samuel 6:8-9, he had been angry and afraid of God for at least three months time as a result of the Lord's wrath against his servant Uzzah. When he finally decided to return to the blessings of God, his spirit was stirred to offer a sacrifice of praise. In addition to the scriptural account of his leaping and jump-

ing, there must have been a most significant amount of spinning and whirling that occurred during King David's praise. In order for him to have come out of his garments, no other physical action could have made such an intense impact as to be described as dancing with 'all his might'.

In our expressions of 'karar', one will find renewed and restored joy if they have first been delivered in their spirits from all inhibitions that would serve to discourage them from obtaining their breakthrough. Other expressions of 'karar' include: **2Samuel 6:14, 2Samuel 6:16, Ecclesiastes 1:6, Isaiah 66:15, Nahum 1:3, Habakkuk 3:14.**

6. NAQAPH: To strike with violence; to encompass; to go round about; to destroy and cut down.

The expression of 'naqaph' describes an action used in both biblical and spiritual warfare. Naqaph allows one to strategize against the enemy for his ultimate demise. In every ministry, particularly the dance ministry, the 'General' or leader, should have a fundamental understanding of military tactics and maneuvers in order for them to properly advise and instruct their 'troops'. The expression of 'naqaph' carries with it a basic principle: **enclose, strike, and destroy**. In cases where the leader is also the head choreographer, he or she must discern the times when the Holy Spirit declares war! If the dance created is to be set choreography, the discerning dance minister will incorporate formations which include **circles** (around the entire space; symbolizes continuous surveillance and protection; surrounds the enemy), strong, **single-file lines** (symbolizing unity), and **'V'-formations** (representing the point of an arrow). Utilizing these formations will also prove effective during spontaneous instruction from the Holy Spirit during the Worship Experience. The *encompassing* should precede all forms of attacks that are to be executed by the ministry during times of warfare.

Whether one surrounds the enemy through prayer and intercession, or one physically manifests the surrounding in the body, adopting this tactic will allow for a common sense of purpose and focus to set in among the dance warriors. Consider the military strategy and positioning of Joshua's army in the battle of Jericho in
Joshua 6:1-5:

> **Then the LORD said to Joshua, "See, I have delivered Jericho into your hands, along with its king and its fighting men. March around the city once with all the armed men. Do this for six days. Have seven priests carry trumpets of rams' horns in front of the ark. On the seventh day, march around the city seven times, with the priests blowing the trumpets, have all the people give a loud shout; then the wall of the city will collapse and the people will go up, every man straight in."**

In times of war, there will also be seasons where the Holy Spirit will call forth certain individuals to encompass their leaders who may be under personal attack themselves or have ministries that are under attack. 2Chronicles 23:4-7 beautifully outlines military instructions given by the priest Jehoiada, whose name means, 'the Lord knows':

> **"Now this is what you are to do: A third of you priests and Levites who are going on duty on the Sabbath are to keep watch at the doors, a third of you at the royal palace, and a third at the Foundation Gate, and all the other men are to be in the courtyards of the temple of the LORD. No one is to enter the temple of the LORD except the priests and Levites on duty;**

they may enter because they are consecrated, but all other men are to guard what the LORD has assigned to them. The Levites are to station themselves around the king, each man with his weapons in his hand. Anyone who enters the temple must be put to death. Stay close to the king wherever he goes."

During the expressions of 'naqaph', the minister must be intentional about their purpose. The movements executed for the striking of the enemy must be aggressive, direct, and meaningful. There is never a time during naqaph for the dance warrior to be 'cute' or 'trite'—this is not a game, rather it is a spiritual battle. Someone's healing, children, financial breakthrough, or their very life may depend on our obedience and precision in movement ministry during this season. Other scriptural references to the expression of 'naqaph' include: **Joshua 6:11, 2Kings 6:14, 2Chronicles 23:7, Psalm 17:9,Psalm 22:16, and Isaiah 10:34.**

Prayer Declaration:

This Is MY BODY and I love it!
I command myself now to lift my hands, wave my arms, twist my body, surround the enemy, and stomp furiously as a Sign that I will no longer allow my body be held captive by my mind, its inhibitions, and its lack of knowledge! Thank you, Father, for new-found liberation with PURPOSE and Understanding in the Name of Jesus!
AMEN.

APPENDIX 2

Sample: Interpretive and Liturgical Dance Level 1 Adult Course Curriculum

The following sample course curriculum is meant to be a guide for establishing biblical and technical foundations within Sacred Dance and Arts ministry teams. This course, or the like, is required for incoming members to the ministry; therefore, it must be successfully completed with a final grade of 'B' or better by the prospective team members prior to their release to minister with the team in a full capacity.

The format, content, and timetable may be adjusted to meet the specific needs of the ministry team. Directors may use this sample curriculum to develop various levels of technique and study for different dance or dramatic forms and styles. These may range from beginners, to intermediate, to advanced level training. The Director may also use the same foundational content, course description, objectives, and goals to modify and create a program for children and young teens.

Sample:	**Introductory Course Curriculum for New Ministry Team Members (Adult Model)**
COURSE NAME:	**Interpretive and Liturgical Dance in Worship (Level 1)**
COURSE YEAR:(	**Season, Year)**
COURSE DURATION:	**15 Weeks**
INSTRUCTOR (S):	**(Name)**

Course Description

Students are instructed on the biblical origin of dance, sacred dance traditions, and the evolution of dance in a worship service or setting. Students are introduced to the interpretive/liturgical dance vocabulary through technical movement demonstration, and Biblical instruction. Students are encouraged to lead as pioneers on the cutting-edge of creativity in the ministry of sacred dance as an open door to missions, global Church transformation, and souls won to Christ. Students are trained to view sacred artistry in the dance as God's universal language, thus being a powerful tool for ministry to all cultures.

Course Goal

- To provide students with the physical, spiritual, and Biblical disciplines of Christian sacred dance.
- To facilitate a process of achieving spiritual deliverance and liberation in worship through movement.
- To prepare students for ministry in missions and evangelism through the artistry of dance.
- To train a new generation of ministers equipped to lead in sacred artistry.
- To educate prospective pastors and church leaders on

the power of congregational worship in the dance.
- To demonstrate effective, biblical principles which allow the incorporation of dance throughout any worship service.
- To equip students to become dance disciples and evangelists to other cultures and Nations.

Course Objectives
- To provide clear definition and understanding of interpretive, sacred, and liturgical dance
- To identify the gifting, burden, and call to dance ministry on an individual's life
- To compel students to complete a self-analysis of their personal lifestyles as it relates to their personal worship experience
- To provide specific spiritual disciplines and requirements for the liturgical/sacred dancer
- To provide a firm foundation [in technical expertise] at a beginner-intermediate level in various forms of dance, including, but not limited to the following: modern, ballet, African, Hebrew, and folk
- To train students as trailblazers on the cutting-edge of creativity in the ministry of dance as an open door to receiving Jesus Christ.
- To bring appreciation and heightened awareness of the unifying power of sacred dance and artistry to cross-cultural and cross-denominational segments of the Church universal.

Course Requirements/Assignments
1. Mid-term exam (20%)
2. Final Exam (25%)
3. Each student (at instructor's discretion) will be expected to demonstrate in dance ministry at least **once per semester** during times of praise and worship,

special ministry engagements, or conferences. (15%)
4. Class and rehearsal attendance will make up (20%) of student's grade.
5. Each student is required to attend and/or view at least one dance presentation (to be approved by instructor). A 3-page typed paper will be completed on the viewing. Other Special Reports or reading assignments may be given at instructor's discretion. (10%)
6. Quizzes will make up (10%) of student's grade.

Other Requirements
- Regular Bible study/discussion group attendance at local church
- Maintenance of a Prayer and Revelations Journal

Please Note:
- Three (3) marks of tardiness from class will result in one (1) mark of absence;
- Three (3) marks of absence from class will result in one (1) letter grade drop.

Resources and Suggested Reading:

The Holy Bible

My Body is the Temple: Encounters and Revelations on Sacred Dance and Artistry
Author: Rev. Stephanie Butler
Xulon Press, 2002

The Three Battlegrounds
Author: Francis Frangipane
Arrow Publications, 1989

I Dance With God
Author: Dr. Cecelia Williams Bryant
AKOSUA Visions, 1995

Here and Now: Living in the Spirit
Author: Henry Nouwen
Crossroad Publishing Co., 1995

We Don't Die, We Kill Ourselves: How to Defeat the Top 10 Killers
Author: Dr. Cris C. Enriquez, M.D.
Christian Services Network, 2000

The Dance of Joy: A Biblical Approach to Praise and Worship
Author: Murray Silberling
Lederer Messianic Publishers, 1995

Sample: Interpretive and Liturgical Dance, Level One Course Schedule

Week:	Dates:	Topic:
1	(TBA)	Preparing the Ground through Prayer and Intercession
		Defining Liturgical Dance
		Biblical Foundation of Dance
		Warm-up and Technique
		Biblical Foundation of Dance
		Hebrew and Greek Word Study of Dance
		Rejoicing in the LORD
2		Quiz #1
		Are You Called to Dance

Mid-Term Exam

8   Integration of Sacred Dance during the Worship Experience

Processionals and Recessionals

Praise and Worship

The Sermonic Dance

Dance of Invitation

Warm-Up and Technique

9   Quiz #4
Dancing Your Prayers

10   Special Reports and Independent Study

11,12   Becoming Dance Disciples through Missions and Evangelism

Warm Up and Technique

13   Garments of Praise, Costuming, and Biblical Colors

Warm Up and Technique

14, 15   Administration and
                               Management of a Dance
                               Ministry

                               Appointing a Leader, and
                               How to Lead a Dance
                               Ministry

                               Review for Final

                               Final Examination

Sample Sacred Arts
Ministry Team
Mission Objectives

In order for any ministry or organization to operate at its full potential effectively, there must be a strong sense of direction and purpose. This is commonly achieved by developing AND adhering to mission goals and objectives. Each ministry team must clearly identify its overall purpose and place as it relates to the way that God has called them to serve. As your Sacred Dance or Arts Ministry team develops, the director or leader must be clear about the direction God is leading, and must be able to verbally articulate the objectives to the team as a whole. The following is just one example of how one set of Mission Objectives may be outlined, with scriptures to accompany them.

Sample: Sacred Arts Ministry Team: Mission Objectives

1) **To live a life of holiness unto the Lord**
   [Scripture(s) Romans 12:1; 1Corinthians 6:19; 1Peter 1:14-16]

2) **To impart the spiritual disciplines and require-ments of service to God through Sacred Artistry by transforming our bodies into weapons of worship, warfare, deliverance and prophetic intercession.**
   [Scripture(s) Romans 1:11; Psalm 18:11; Judges 3:1-2; Revelations 15:4; 1Timothy 2:1-7]

3) **To operate under a global anointing to train, disci-ple, and equip men, women and children to minis-ter the Gospel by combining 21st Century missions strategies with the Performing Arts.**
   [Scripture(s) Matthew 28:18-20; Mark 16:15-16]

4) **To maintain divine order within the ministry team structure so that prayer life, study, rehearsal schedules and ministry obligations are understood and adhered to.**
   [Scripture(s) 1Corinthians 14:40; Romans 5:19]

5) **To identify the Call to Sacred Artistry in both pro-fessional and non-professional artists by teaching them to make the connection between movement and gesture, biblical text, and their Christian expe-rience in order to actualize God's message to the Body of Christ.**
   [Scripture(s) Ephesians 1:18; 2Peter 1:10]

6) **To be multi-national in ministry of songs, cultural**

dances, and productions in the presentation of the Gospel.
[Scripture(s) Isaiah 66:18; Revelations 15:4]

Sample: Prospective Ministry Team Member Interview/Questionnaire

The following questions may be conducted via round-table interview, hardcopy, or a combination of the two. The latter is most preferred and recommended. The reason for this combination is that doing so will allow the prospective members a chance to express themselves verbally and in written form. This is helpful to the leaders, directors, in further identifying the spiritual maturity and ability to articulate clearly and reasonably.

1. Are you a born-again Believer?

2. When did you accept Jesus Christ as your personal Lord and Savior?

3. Please tell about your conversion experience.

4. Are you currently an active member of a Bible-believing local church?

5. What kind of Christian service or ministries are you presently active in at your local church?

6. What kind of Christian service or ministries are you presently active in outside of your local church?

7. Are you aware of a definite call of God to a particular ministry on your life? Describe it.

8. Tell what previous experience, professional or otherwise, that you have in any specific discipline of the Arts.

9. How often do you attend Bible study or Bible discussion groups? Sunday school?

10. Are you filled with the Holy Spirit? If yes, describe why you believe this is true.

11. What is your perception of ministry versus 'performance'?

12. Specifically, why do you want to be a part of this particular ministry?

13. Aside from your specific skill in your area of discipline, what characteristics would you bring to the ministry team?

APPENDIX 5

Testimonials

The following are statements of testimony to the power of the sacred dance experience and what it has meant in the lives of both current and past students who have dedicated their bodies in praise, worship, and warfare unto the Lord.

"Praising the Lord in dance makes me feel free and strong. There is a freedom in my spirit and oftentimes there is a natural progression to do warfare in the dance. I feel like I could actually fly, jumping so high in the air, and just not wanting to stop even though my body might be crying out to stop! I feel like there is no mountain too high or no problem too big that I can't overcome it—Through dance I am an Overcomer"!

—Ms. Dulsie Johnson, student—Jamaica

"My view of African people and their culture has been greatly enhanced by having taken this course in African Praise Dance. I recognize that we can all honor and glorify God within our cultural, traditional style of music and dance. Seeing that the African tradition has a very spiritual connection and a lot to do with war, preparation for war, but also that these are a people of much celebration. I learned that they [Africans] had a fighting spirit as a result of years of physical enslavement, but that their music and dance helped to free their minds from mental slavery. There is definitely a fight in my spirit and much exuberant joy when praising the Lord with African music".

—Ms. Dana Morrison, student—Jamaica

"My experience through taking this course on liturgical dance has taught me a lot about myself and about my nation. I learned that what I wear must give honor and dignity to myself and to God. The garments must be unique, beautiful, and priestly. I ministered in liturgical dance when I went back home to South Africa at a conference. The theme was, "Africa, Arise and Lead", so there were leaders from the different nations of Africa. I knew from the minute I started [dancing] that the Spirit of God had taken over. By the time I was done dancing, the people were just worshipping all over. When liturgical dancers allow the Spirit of God to work through them, the anointing will flow, and people will be convicted of their sins".

—Miss Ade Bam, student—South Africa

"Before, I never attended any kind of dance class. When I made the decision to take the class, it was a pleasure, but it was very hard. I could not move my body exactly how I felt that my body should move! I was even considering leaving the class at once. But, now, I feel comfortable. [Dancing] is one of the things that has challenged my life, and believe it or not, helped me to discover my purpose. When I am in the presence of the Lord, I feel a passion to express myself in dance. When I am praising the Lord, I realized that it is the movements that made me feel the Spirit of the Lord manifest in my life. When you go into the presence of the Lord, like dancing, you cannot stay only in one place. You have to move. I wonder if every Believer can see that"?

—Mr. Jean Daniel, student—Haiti

"During my courses, I have ministered to God through Hip-Hop, Reggae, African and liturgical dance. When I am dancing, I believe that I touch the heart of God. Especially through African Praise, I experience freedom, peace, and lightness of feet. When I dance, I imagine that my Father stops, watches me, stamps His feet, and says, "Go, Nicolette, go!" He enjoys seeing me arrest and chase away the enemy. The knowledge of this fills me with much happiness and joy".

—Miss Nicollette Simms, student—Jamaica

"As a pastor in training, I have learned how liturgical dance can impact nations. In dance, we are encouraged to express what God has done in our lives—this is how we can minister to Him. We have communion with God through open expressions of worship and praise. I can see how we can also evangelize with our bodies through dance. For me, liturgical dance has opened me up from being shy and a bit reclusive in showing what [good] God has been. This has changed my life [because] I feel more free, alive, and powerful when I dance and when I speak [preach]. I will use what I have learned to evangelize to the nations".

—Mr. Hugh Murray, student—Jamaica

"I was thankful for learning about this form of expression. I am a psalmist for my church, but I also love to dance. Through the teaching on the real meaning of liturgical dance, it has allowed me to feel the words of the songs that I sing to God even more deeply. Before the teaching, our church had never experienced dancing as a congregation during praise and worship. It was a very new thing to us, and

I interceded a lot for this specifically. I know it was the work of the Holy Spirit that allowed us to sing in Chinese as [you] interpreted the dance in the Spirit. When I looked out and saw our people following in the movements, I was over-joyed".

—Mrs. Cathy Chang, student/workshop participant—Taiwan

"In most nations, there are 'religious' or 'holy' people who think dance is for heathens. If I continue in the dance ministry, the more I dance, the more barriers will be broken and the anointing will open the eyes of these 'holy' people so they may see into the spirit realm—they will see God dance".

—Miss Deneice Wedderburn, student—Jamaica

"In the course on liturgical dance, I learned why scriptures such as Romans 12:1 and 1Corinthians 6:19 are essential to every sacred dancer. Our bodies are important to God. They are really His temple, or dwelling place. For us as dancers, it is also our ministry tool, that's why it must first of all be holy. Nobody will drink out of a filthy cup or like to dwell in a filthy house. [My body] has to be holy...it is my sacrifice to God and I must take care of it".

—Mr. Quincy Girigorie, student—Curacão

"I love dancing and ministering to God through dance. I know that one day, a great multitude will stand before God—that includes people from every nation, tribe, and language, giving glory to God. I believe that in heaven we will be free to praise God in our own cultural expressions. I believe in heaven there will be opera, jazz, classical, and reggae music to name a few. As long as it's holy! I see myself standing with an African/Caribbean group who will worship God while beating Congo drums, contracting and releasing as fast as we can! When I sing hymns and sway to the keyboard, I do feel full of adoration and reverence for God. This is wonderful, but it is when I begin to leap around to the beat of drums that I feel as if I am releasing myself to do something I was created to do. It is because of the blood running through my veins that I feel a burst of gratitude to God that is best expressed by me when my feet move fast! I am sure it is because God made me so".

—Miss Paulette Kelly, student—USA/Jamaica

CPSIA information can be obtained
at www.ICGtesting.com
Printed in the USA
LVOW03s0101191017

552967LV00003B/163/P